CW00829724

Visual

Manifest Your Dream With More Clarity
Using Imagination And Brain Training

*(Achieve Limitless Success And Improve Your Life
With Visualization Exercises)*

Todd Woodhouse

Published By **Jennifer Windy**

Todd Woodhouse

Visualization: Manifest Your Dream With More Clarity Using Imagination And Brain Training (Achieve Limitless Success And Improve Your Life With Visualization Exercises)

ISBN 978-1-77485-629-1

Legal & Disclaimer

The information contained in this ebook is not designed to replace or take the place of any form of medicine or professional medical advice. The information in this ebook has been provided for educational & entertainment purposes only.

The information contained in this book has been compiled from sources deemed reliable, and it is accurate to the best of the Author's knowledge; however, the Author cannot guarantee its accuracy and validity and cannot be held liable for any errors or omissions. Changes are periodically made to this book. You must consult your doctor or get professional medical advice before using any of the suggested remedies, techniques, or information in this book.

Upon using the information contained in this book, you agree to hold harmless the Author from and against any damages, costs, and expenses, including any legal fees potentially

Table of Contents

Chapter 1: Meditation For Creative Visualization

The ability to manage, create and project images is called creative visualization. Creative visualization can improve physical and mental sight.

Because visualization is a cognitive act, it is well-suited for helping people overcome negative thoughts. These include anxiety, depressions, low motivation, creative blocks, exacerbating anxiety and depression. Long-standing metaphysical and esoteric traditions have shown that creative visualization can be an important tool in spiritual growth. It is also fundamental to the realization of our desires.

It's possible to use creativity for our benefit:

Reach challenging goal

Increase creativity and concentration

Use our mind to train our body

Faster learning

Change our self-image

We can do almost anything we imagine.

Although our minds are wired to think and create, we may not be aware of it. The best way to control your life is to train your brain to create positive imagery. It will be easy to recognize and achieve our goals by practicing regular visualization.

Only meditation and creative visualization will make our dreams become a reality.

It's not possible to be positive and visualize our dreams. If we have parts within us that think it's impossible to achieve our dreams or doubt our abilities or fears of success, it will make it difficult for us to focus on our purpose. These parts or elements in us only contribute to making life extremely difficult. We must fight to think positively in order to stop these parts from trying to think negatively.

We cannot just overcome our fears by relying on positive thinking to get to where you want to be.

Creative Visualization Meditation, however, is still very useful. It gives us clues on what to do next in order to make the dreams come true.

What creative visualization meditation does for us is to bring us into alignment with the dream. This is very good. If we want to see our dream come to life, it must be in our energy. Creative visualization meditation is an effective tool.

Sometimes we just try to align with our dreams. This makes it very easy to see where we are and how we are not in alignment with our dreams.

It points out the need to heal and transform before we can attain what we want.

This means that we should pay attention to the feelings and thoughts that are triggered by creative visualizations and keep a log of them. This is what you need to know before you can take your next step towards your dream.

Creative visualization meditation offers many benefits.

Meditation has become a popular way to unwind, relax, increase spiritual growth, and improve your quality of life in this busy, modern world.

Meditation is gaining popularity because of its many positive effects.

Listening to guided meditations can be a simple way to feel the benefits of meditation.

It's Effortless!

Meditation is an enjoyable, healthy, and inspiring method to attain inner peace. Guided Meditations are, quite simply speaking, the easiest way for one to meditate.

Traditional meditation techniques that are not guided, although they can be quite beautiful, require some effort. It is our responsibility keep your mind clear, focused, and clear. With guided meditation, however, we are guided to a place of meditation through spoken word guidance. Our guide will help us walk through the steps step by step.

Is there anything more easy and relaxing than listening peaceful music while we are guided to deep meditation?

Guided Meditation is not only simple but also powerful in helping you to grow personally.

Meditation plus visualization

Guided meditations are a great way to visualize.

Guided meditations make life interesting, as they allow us to use the power our imagination and visualize positive changes. This is why guided meditations have a greater impact than passive meditation.

Visualization, or creative visualization, is the process of using mental imagery and mental imagery in order to create positive changes within our lives. Visualization techniques are used widely in many fields like the arts, business and spirituality, as well psychotherapy and self improvement.

Denis Waitley, coach to the Olympic champions and Apollo astronauts, once said:

"The mind is unable to distinguish between a real, life-like event and a vividly imaginable one."

Guided meditations are a way to visualise positive experiences and express any changes you wish to make in your life.

Guided meditation places us in such a state that our imagery becomes vivid and clearer. It's a blissful experience to be immersed in guided meditation while listening for positive suggestions. We feel better in all aspects of our lives, whether they are physical, spiritual, or emotional.

A well-crafted guided meditation will often include positive suggestions, positive visualizations, and other positive thoughts that allow us to experience the inner changes we are looking for in our outer lives.

Why is creative visualization meditation so crucial? Let's give The Buddha the opportunity to answer this question:

"The mind can change everything." What you think about is what you become.

Guided meditations enable us to attain a state that is deep within stillness. Our mind can then be clear of unwanted thoughts and clutter, and then we can experience vivid visualization experiences that drive positive personal transformations.

Guided meditations, especially those that are particularly well-crafted, may use symbolic imagery in order to connect with our deeper, more abstract minds. This helps to facilitate profound healing and personal development.

Creative visualization exercise

These advanced exercises will enable us to create vivid visualizations. These advanced exercises will demonstrate how to produce stronger feelings and emotions through visualizations or improve the effectiveness of our visualizations.

These ideas will enable us to dramatically improve the results that we see through a simple and powerful shift of perspective. If we want to achieve a specific outcome or attain a particular goal, but have difficulty and frustration getting there, then this is the right place to read. It takes only a few simple steps to improve your visualization and speed up your progress.

Although advanced visualization techniques can be quite simple, it is still important to understand the basics of visualization.

Advanced Visualization Exercise 2: Speak it loud

"Everything will be a little more interesting if it is spoken loudly." "-Hermann Hesse

Talking to yourself via visualization is a great way of making things more vivid. Our minds can wander sometimes when we visualize and end up consuming irrelevant information. This can make it difficult to visualize clearly and reduce the effectiveness of your results. Some people have difficulties visualizing crisp, clear images. These tasks can be accomplished more easily with advanced visualization. This visualization exercise requires that you simply speak out what is happening in your head or the things we desire. Simple!

As we imagine the situation, we are simply able to mutter what's going and how to feel. We must remember that visualization success depends on the ability to generate the right feelings. Therefore, we should talk to ourselves through emotions.

It's really as simple as saying that you own your business. I am proud of my employees, who work hard and enjoy being here. My customers are my most valued customers. I'm making a lot for what I love. I feel amazing. I'm confident, powerful, and overall successful. It is good!

Just by saying it outloud, we can improve the clarity of our vision and increase the intensity the emotions we produce.

Simply speak all that you feel or see and it will come out.

It will be clear that our imagination will produce vivider, brighter and more focused images. We will feel more emotions. They will also be stronger. Overall, it will be easier for us all to stay on track.

Advanced Visualization Exercise 2: No ego allowed

"It is possible to see beyond the boundaries of wrong-doings and right-doings. There is a field. I'll meet up with you there" --Rumi

To be able to visualize the next challenging exercise, we need to shift our thinking.

You can't expect the outcome to be perfect when you use creative visualization.

This means we can't attach anything to the achievement of our goals. We cannot depend on the results of visualization being realized.

In other words, we must not see any hidden motives in the achievement of our goals. It's important that we can visualize our desired outcome without any hidden motives and experience what it would feel like.

Simply watch the video to see how it feels to achieve your goals.

Happiness doesn't come from achieving results. That's it. This is the key. No ego allowed!

Advanced Visualization Exercise 3

"We only can be considered alive when our hearts are aware that our treasures are within our reach" -Thornton Wilder

We were, quite frankly, a very unhappy person. We could not see any good in this life.

You should always be focused on what you don't have and the things that you want, not what you do have. Life was, for the most parts, a massive effort. It was difficult to get through everything.

We didn't realize that we were vibrant and healthy, with great friendships, loving families, good food and a great place to live. Multiple cycles of depression and misery were common.

Advanced Visualization exercise 4: Use binauralbeats

Binaural beats can be used to reduce anxiety, stress, and improve focus and self-confidence.

Sounds like a miracle cure. They work miracles, even though they sound too good for it.

Binaural beats can be used to practice visualization exercises, if that's possible. Binaural beat technology makes visualization much easier than it used to be. It is not a costly investment that will be repaid many times over by the wonderful results.

The first benefit is the faster we can relax than other relaxation techniques. We will feel deep relaxation and peace within two to three mins depending on the binaural beats package we use. The muscles and bodies will be relaxed, and we will begin to drift off. It's sort of like a nap and everyone loves a nap.

It is important to feel relaxed when visualizing. Binaural beats accomplish this task faster than any other method. It saves time every time we visualize, and allows us more often to visualize. The best way to get more results is to visualize!

Advanced Visualization: 5: Practice

For advanced visualization exercises, this is it.

Visualizations should be spoken aloud. This will allow us to express our gratitude and to visualize with no ego.

These techniques do work. We don't know how they work. These techniques have proven to be extremely effective in transforming lives. Many of these people have experienced dramatic changes in their lives. As with all abilities, the more we visualize, we become better at it. We can have fun with this by picturing ourselves succeeding. This brings us the pure joy, thrill, happiness and satisfaction of all the things we had previously imagined.

Chapter 2: The Law Of Attraction: Attracting Wealth, Money And Abundance

Similar to how you used the law to attract love to you, you can also use this same principle to attract wealth to your life.

Create your wealth and abundance boards and start practicing visualizations and positive affirmations. This will help you attract more money. You can also make these practices a part of your daily life to increase the speed at which you bring money, wealth, abundance, and prosperity into your life.

Get specific about the type and amount of wealth and money you want.

First, be clear about how much money you want and how much abundance you would like. Is it your dream to be a millionaire and/or do you want to have enough money to allow your family to live comfortably? Do you like living from one paycheck into the next or do your financial goals include freedom from any financial constraints? This clarity can help you identify exactly the kind of wealth, abundance, & money you desire and focus your efforts on it.

Clearly define the amount that you desire in your bank accounts if you are aiming to have a specific amount. Do you want to become a millionaire, a billionaire or just make a couple hundred dollars each month? If you aren't clear about how much you want to earn, you will have a vague goal that will not allow you to give clear instructions.

Once you're clear about what kind of wealth and abundance your dream of, create a financial- and abundance-related goal that is based on it. Create a wealth board to support your goal. Place it on a prominent place in your house, preferably the upper left of your house. It is the Feng Shui location for wealth. Keep the wealth board up for 15 minutes every day. Use it to visualize your goal and practice affirmations based upon wealth, money, abundance.

Here are some suggestions.

"I have fulfilled my financial goal and am living a happy life."

"I attract abundance, wealth, and prosperity easily and it helps me live an amazing and fulfilling life."

"I find it easier than to draw money towards myself and my banking account is always healthy."

"I have an abundance mindset. This helps me attract more wealth to myself."

Develop a Abundance Mindset

An abundance mindset is one that encourages you to have abundance and live a full life. This will help you attract more. Start to feel more grateful for what you have and less about where you need to be. Being grateful for all the blessings in your life will make you happy and help you feel more fulfilled. This will align your vibrational frequency with the universe, allowing you to draw more wealth and abundance toward yourself.

You can do this by waking up and writing about 3-5 things that are important to you. Thank the universe for these blessings and elaborate on their importance. So that you end the day positive and thankful, be sure to go over this account before bed. It is possible to thank the universe, for instance, for granting you a house to call home, a steady income, and for providing a comfortable bed for you to sleep in.

Your happiness will increase if you place more emphasis on your blessings everyday. This doesn't mean to stop striving for wealth and prosperity. You should let go any previous complaining attitudes and adopt a more content attitude.

You feel happy with your life. This allows you to keep striving for excellence but with more positivity. This will help you feel happier about your life. You can also work harder to achieve your goals.

Also, before you go to sleep, say a wealth-related affirmation. This will help you keep your mind focused on your wealth goal even when it isn't. Do this every day. You'll feel more at ease and be able to focus on your wealth-related goals.

Calm Your Inner Critic

If your inner critic is telling you how you will never be able to achieve your wealth-related goals, it is hard for you to focus on them. Your inner critic refers to the negative inner voice that you have a tendency to hear. You might try focusing your attention on your wealth and a affirmation, such as "I'm a millionaire." This will cause your inner critic to speak negatively about you. It is likely to happen more than once, but you have to fight it.

Being aware of your inner critic is a good way to do this. You should be gentle and kind when you hear it saying negative things about you. Let it go and say, "Thank you," then quickly change that suggestion towards something more encouraging. If it reads, "How are you going to become a millionaire?" you could modify it to say, "If it's possible, I can earn more than a thousand dollars per month."

Realistic ideas such as the ones above will calm your inner critic. You can then think positively and keep your eyes on your goal. Keep doing this for a few times, and you'll soon be able to cultivate a positive mindset and stop your inner critic from getting in the way.

Keep your bank account topped up

If your bank balance is low and often empty, it will make it hard to attract money. Just as you need to be positive to attract positive experiences in your life, so too must you have money. It won't help to draw more money into your lives if you have a low bank balance.

Try these tips to achieve this.

1. First, you need to be clear on what your expenses are and how much you can afford. Next, make sure that you only spend on the essentials.

2. You should take into consideration your earnings. If they are lower than your basic expenses you need to make ends meet, then look for ways that you can make more.

3. Earn even a fraction more than your essential expenses and save some of it, even if it is only $5

4. Every week, set yourself a goal to save $5 to $15 and to increase that amount by $5 every second week. Slowly, your savings fund will grow and you will be able to keep it safe. 50% of the money can be used (when it grows large enough) to put into a good savings program. The remainder can then be deposited in your bank account and used to increase its value.

5. Slowly reduce impulse buying in order to save more.

6. Do not be in debt. You will only attract more debt. You can use your savings to repay debt. When you are finally debt free, start saving more so the money you save can be used to bring more money into your financial life.

These hacks will help you achieve wealth faster if you start to work on them immediately.

Eliminate all Fears and Limitations that May Prevent You from Realizing Your Goal

It's OK to have some doubts about the fulfillment or abundance of your money and wealth goals. If you allow these fears to fester, it can hinder your progress and make it harder to reach your goals.

Banish these fears so that this doesn't happen.

1. All the reasons you feel scared or that you won't be able to achieve the wealth and success you desire. You may believe that your credit score is not as good as you would like and you won't be able this time to reach your financial goals.

2. Think about each fear one-by-one and try to understand its root cause. What are the reasons you keep this fear alive?

3. Ask yourself questions that will help determine if a fear is true. If you think that you have always been a failure ask yourself: "Was the last time I accomplished something?" Your mind will then bring up examples that will prove that you are capable. It is important to ask positive questions of yourself. Because your mind always answers the same question as you

do, it will also answer it positively. Asking yourself the question, "Will you fail?" will give you many reasons to believe that it is true. The question "Will I fail?" will provide you with more reasons to believe you can succeed. Ask positive questions of yourself to increase your self-belief.

4. Once you know the root cause, resolve the problem positively. Focus on the end goal and talk positively to your self.

5. Furthermore, think of the best ways to achieve your goal. Then start to follow these steps. Success and confidence are built by living the life you live. It is not enough to dream of being successful. You must actually work towards that goal. Make a determination and keep it. Keep to your plan of attack and keep it up so that you can get closer towards your goal. By doing this, you can build your self-confidence. The law of attraction states that success attracts like.

Live as if your Wealth is Yours

You must act as if money is yours to attract it. Your subconscious will accept your wealth and you will feel wealthy. Your subconscious cannot tell the real from the imaginary, so if your subconscious keeps telling you that you have achieved something great, it will continue to bring you similar experiences.

Grant Cardone has been a top sales trainer, speaker, author, social media personality, business innovator, and international speaker. He believes strongly in LOA. In an interview, Cardone mentioned that he used travel to housing societies to inspect houses that he wanted to live in. This was when he began to dream of becoming wealthy. He still thought about these houses and felt as though he had the wealth to buy everything he wanted. This only made him more determined to accomplish his goal.

To reach your goal, you must follow the example of others. Increase your visits to high-end shops; attend more open house events in the communities you live in; test drive expensive cars at car dealerships; find a charity to which you would like a large donation; search for education and businesses; and do other similar activities with your money. If you make positive changes to how you see money, and start to think differently about it, you will begin to see the results you are looking for.

You can be happy with the state of your current money

All of these things should be taken into consideration, but you must also consider being content with your current financial situation. Yes, it can be hard to be happy with what you don't have, but that doesn't mean you won't feel peaceful about your own life. You cannot attract abundance and wealth to yourself if your life is not peaceful.

Start being grateful for your current financial position. To be able to receive more and better, you must appreciate what you have. Do not be ashamed to admit that you may be bankrupt. This is an amazing blessing. Accept it first and work your way up to the wealth you want.

Every day, open your wallet. This will make you happy with your finances and enable you to create more wealth for yourself. A red wallet is a good idea. You should add a small amount each day to it. Every object and each color has its own power. You will attract similar objects and colors to yourself. Red is associated both with wealth, abundance, and a red wallet/bag draws more money your way. Imagine more money entering your bag if you have money. Imagine many $100 bills flowing through the same $10 bill you kept in it. You can use this visualization to attract more money by activating a RAS.

Finally, you can give the money in your wallet every day or weekly to someone in crisis. You can help others by giving to charity. Also, it will bring you better things. This is a great way for you to show your gratitude to the universe.

Consistency is key to success. Keep working on these strategies consistently. Your belief system will bring you money.

Now let's look at how to make the next chapter successful.

Chapter 3: Get Started Meditating

You may be wondering why so many people feel drawn to meditation. You see, meditation can relax you and help to drive stress away. If you meditate in the morning, this will ensure that you feel relaxed for the rest the day. You'll also be able and capable of doing what you need to do with ease. Meditation increases heart rate, metabolism, prevents sleeplessness, normalizes bloodpressure, and improves heart health.

Meditation should be part of your daily practice. A few minutes of meditation is sufficient. You can even stay there for up to 30 or more minutes.

It's best to meditate in the early morning as the mind is known to be calmer than other times of day. You must meditate on a regular basis. This will help you to be more self-reliant.

Here are some excellent ways to meditate.

You can choose the space you want. Find a quiet area in your home to place a cushion, a mat or other items. Others may create their own altars using candles and inspirational photographs. This is entirely up to you. Be sure to keep your space private and away from others.

Make sure you are sitting correctly. If you're trying to meditate, sit down on the floor or on an ottoman/mat. Allow your hands to rest on your lap. Close your eyes.

Breathe. Meditation is also all about learning to relax, and how to breathe freely. Your neck, stomach, hands, and face should be relaxed. Then breathe through your nose. Try to relax and soften your body, and let go all tension.

Be clear about where you want to focus your attention. The object of meditation doesn't necessarily need to be something tangible. It can be one of these things:

Unleash your body's natural sensations

The rising and descending of the chest, your hands feeling, or any body changes that happen as you breathe.

Your breath is what leaves and enters your nostrils.

You may hear sounding from outside, or from your body.

This will help you focus on meditation rather than worrying about what your day should look like. Concentrate on this "object" for at most ten breaths, then take another deep breath and start again.

Choose your Mantra. You need to repeat your mantra every day until you believe in it. This will keep you positive all day. Some mantras you could choose are:

I am at Peace

I am happy

I am beautiful

May I be filled up with loving kindness

May love rule my life

May I see the positive side of life

My dreams are possible

I will be successful

You can create your own mantra. It doesn't really matter what mantra you choose, as long as it is positive. Because it will help make your life dreams come true. Repeat these words until your heart is full of them.

You can choose to imagine a sanctuary you call home, or a dream destination you want to visit. Visualize the sea and pretend to be there if it's something you enjoy. Imagine yourself walking on cobblestoned paths through Paris, if you really want to. It will calm you down and make you feel more peaceful.

Chapter 4: Visualization

You should focus your thoughts on the things of the heavens and not on those that are here. (Colossians 3:2)

We have talked about our purpose, desires and goals. Now it's time to figure out how to enhance them and live in harmony with God and His principles. To get the best out our selves, and remain on the path towards happiness and faith, there are proven techniques that we will be learning.

As we said in the previous section, visualize yourself as an sphere. This was a visualization technique. Its function is to enhance your motivation towards healthier desires, in order for them become externalized healthy habits.

This technique can help you calm down and relax, remove any stress elements from your mind, and concentrate on the important things in your life. Our brain is overwhelmed with information. Companies make a big deal of misleading us with modern marketing techniques. They use advertisements to bombard our brains and then sell them false information.

Visualize your ultimate goal and remember it every day. Remember to ask yourself why do you want that or that? And what is your true desire. Regain authorship. God will shine His Will upon yours if it is high in its vibration. Prayer, constant thoughtfulness of our true wants, being present in every moment and focusing upon the goal can help us get rid of daily stress.

You must remember that all external manifestations are always based on an internal basis. It's rooted in your souls and processed within your mind. Tune into your higher vibrations and God's frequency. Clear, honest and sincere desires are more likely to lead to greater and better outcomes than those that aren't true. Realizing that God has the power to empower you to make this world a better place and to be His tool allows you to feel happy.

To put it another way, positive affirmations can be used daily to literally hack your mind. This technique can easily be empowered with the help prayers. Use the power of daily affirming your true desires at each end of your prayer. Tell yourself in the presence Providence how you desire to benefit your sisters or brethren. Your message will be selfconsciously accepted as long as you continue to tell yourself this every day. Visualize your goal as you communicate it with the Higher Powers. You'll feel it materializing and being honored. I promise you that your desires will be realized if they are genuine and you act with faith.

Divinity is everywhere. To help you better understand the preceding paragraphs, here's another example:

Imagine that the Voices of God are a tune. Now, we have to learn how to sing along. To be able sing along and be in tune naturally, we must be talented singers. To sum it all, good musicians and singers practice a lot. In our example, the World is God's personal band, and each one of us is a singer for Him. If we show integrity and good faith in all we do, we can bring harmony to the World. We can also inspire others by being 'good musicians'.

Another technique is gratitude. Every day, in writing, you should state why you're grateful for what you have. Count your blessings, for short. Remember God and be grateful for the moment. Remember that you are alive. Be thankful that the Light of Life shines through all of you and warms every part of you. Reflection and reflection on your past experiences of sorrow can help you to move on with your life. Visualize your sphere, or sphere, of light as an integral part of a larger, infinite, and unimaginable whole. But feel it just like you feel the stars as you gaze up at the night sky.

Visualization is one key requirement for achieving your dreams and goals. Keep in mind that each element of the Universe God created has an unseen correspondence. These seeds can be planted with sufficient care and attention to help you achieve your highest goal.

Chapter 5: Attract Love And Wealth

Attracting love or wealth is one thing that many people struggle with in life. Because the person hasn't really used the law to attract and really thought about what they want, these two areas won't be mastered. We can be too vague about what we want in this area and we will never achieve it. You have the power to be specific. Start writing down what you want, and then focus on that every day.

This kind of situation can stop you from moving forward with your life. It only takes time to really think about what you want. The universe won't attract it, so it won't often happen. It will attract the situation you are currently in. If your focus is on this, it will only attract it. The universe will simply answer your questions, I am your command.

These two areas of the life are essential to master. Many people only master one. You're meant not to be limited to one area. Every day you should get excited about the possibilities for your life, and strive to live it every day.

Visualization should look like you are watching the perfect movie, over and over. It's like watching a movie about someone else. Instead of seeing a movie about you, you can close you eyes and look at your own movie. This will allow you to keep dreaming about your perfect movie over and over again.

I would choose to watch my life instead of a movie at the theatres. When your life begins to get exciting, it's the right choice. Clients I have advised to visualise the desired results in their lives have rung me up to tell me small stories.

Change your environment to make yourself the person you want. To become rich, you should keep $300 in your purse so that each time you look for cash it reminds your brain that there is more.

The best way to attract your desired things is by cutting out magazines and hanging them on your wall. Focus on the car you desire and your brain will discover ways to attract it.

You can write down the ideal partner for you if your are single. Write down all the details about your partner, such as their appearance, how they sound, their love life, and their personality. If you love your partner and want to feel more affection, write everything you like about them. You'll be able to visualize your perfect life with them.

Start writing down how much you want to make in 3 months. 6 months. and 1 year. It's important to get specific numbers and be focused on them every day. You don't have to know the exact steps to reach your goal. All you have to do to attract it is to put your focus on it.

There are so many stories about people becoming single and finding the partner of their dreams. There are many people who have made the same money as they wrote down and they don't even realize it.

Imagine you had everything that you wanted. You have to trust the outcome, even if you haven't achieved it before. Just imagine if you desire a particular car in a car shop. It doesn't seem like the car isn't real. Remember, if your desire it, and you believe it can be your reality, then it will attract to you.

Chapter 6: How To Tap Into Your Subconsciousness With 8 Simple Steps

First, tap into the intelligence, wisdom and knowledge that the sub-consciousness offers. Before you can do any programming on it, it is necessary to first learn how the subconscious part of your brain works naturally. You will find it difficult to tap into the sub-conscious first few times. Once you are proficient with the basics, you will be able to program and harness your incredible abilities.

Tapping into Your Sub-conscious 101

1. A vision of where and how you want your life to be is important.

Want to be promoted to the most desirable executive position in your company? If you are interested in being promoted, and reap the benefits of that job, think about how it would feel. Vision, within the context of your sub-conscious, is something you visualize and consider. You need to have a vision that drives you so much to succeed, you won't mind stepping on others' toes. Dreaming about something of epic proportions will motivate you to work hard for your goals, no matter what obstacles might come your way. Even if your mind is overwhelmed by too many tasks, you will find a way to focus and keep your vision alive.

2. Meditation can be included in your daily routine

Meditation is one way to make a connection between the subconscious and conscious parts. It allows you to enter a state known as conscious sleep, where you have the energy and creativity to tap into your subconscious. To tap into your subconsciousness or deal with it, you must be patient. Therefore, a state that allows you to relax and remain still, while keeping your mind free of distractions, can help you access the hidden parts of the iceberg. Experts recommend that your meditation should not exceed one minute for each year. This means you will need to meditate for half an hours if 30 years of age.

Meditation isn't just about sitting in silence, closing your eyes, thinking nothing, but it also involves finding a peaceful place to meditate. There are proper ways to meditate and to breathe to achieve relaxation and stillness. These will be discussed later in this chapter.

3. As much as possible, visualize

Visualize your vision from Step 1, then imagine how you will achieve it. You will be amazed at how easy it is for you to complete that one project that will make a difference in your promotion. Think about the applause that you receive after your name has been called, as well as the many congratulations. Do not just imagine once a week. It's important that you do this daily to prepare for that promotion.

4. Believe that it is possible.

Anything that makes you doubtful, anxious, or negatively motivated will hinder your ability to make your dreams a reality. Consider how easy it is to become discouraged if only a few seconds are spent thinking about the "what Ifs" and what could happen if you do this or another. Let's take, for instance, a man who wants make a good first impression. His confidence will fall if he contemplates the possibility of people not liking him or seeing his flaws. What good will that do?

5. Keep positive thoughts and positive self-talk in mind

Remember that the subconscious cannot process negatives. The sub-conscious cannot process negatives, including the words 'not' as discussed in Chapter 1. This is why it is important to promote positive thinking and happy and harmonious thoughts. Your sub-consciousness is more likely to nurture positive thoughts. If you find it difficult to stay positive all the times, then develop positive self-talk. Self-talk allows you to question, analyze, and otherwise muse about the constant flow in thoughts through your mind. Positive thoughts will flow through your sub-conscious if you are positive about anything and everything.

6. Avoid distractions and limitations

It is important that your goal does not have a time limit. It is okay to accept that things will happen when they are meant to. Your consciousness can be used to erase time frames you have created in your daily life.

It'd also be a great idea to try not to absorb any unnecessary noises from those around you. You can focus on what matters most and remove anything that isn't.

7. Keep in touch and tune with your inner self

Intuitive ideas are self-sending messages sent by your sub-conscious to your consciousness. Listen to your intuitions and take action when appropriate. You can pursue a hobby that is interesting and draws out your creative side to help you find your inner self.

8. Sleep is a great way to bring out the best memories in your head.

Instead of going to sleep worrying and worrying about your life, think about a positive memory you have and relive it until you fall back asleep. This will enable you to connect with the sub-conscious, and immediately create a positive sensation. Once you've anchored your attention on one positive experience, begin counting back from 100 slowly. Tell yourself at each number something that is positive, such "I love me" or "I am more relaxed". The goal is for positive thoughts to be planted in your brain.

How to Meditate Correctly

Meditation is a key to being in-touch and connected with your subconsciousness. But you need the right tips and tricks to get there.

Think of something you want to meditate upon.

Find a quiet place where you can meditate.

No matter whether you are on the floor or in a chair, choose the most comfortable seating position.

Cross your legs and close your eye. This will stop all inner or exterior chatter.

You should focus your attention and your mind on the point in between your eyebrows.

Your breathing is an indicator of how you feel. You can then transcend your mind which is full both good and bad thoughts. Proper breathing is about being aware that you are actually exhaling/inhaling naturally. To do it right, it will take some practice, but eventually you'll be able to do it without too much thought.

To achieve total relaxation with no inner and outer chatter.

Pay attention to your goal or intention. That will help you impress your subconscious mind with your intention.

When you master meditation, it is possible to not only tap into your subconsciousness but also heal your whole body. When you meditate, you may feel discomfort in particular parts of the body. Self-suggestion is one possible treatment.

How to immediately relax through your breathing

Inhale through the nose

Take a deep inhale for three seconds and then let your breath go.

Feel the air moving into your stomach. With your stomach expanding, you will actually feel it.

Feel the air rising up to your lungs by focusing on your stomach.

For 5 seconds, exhale through your mouth.

Rinse again

Chapter 7: Deciding Which Manifests To Make

The expression "You can do whatever you put your head to" leads us to believe that all you have is an idea of what you want and a task to accomplish it. We will then wait for your success.

This is true to some extent. Focused intention coupled with action is a powerful force. This statement is misleading since it doesn't mention that focusing your thoughts on a particular goal can be difficult and even impossible.

What do you really want?

Most people don't know what they want. We believe we do, however we truly do not. We only know the things we don't want. We don't wish for an impossible job. We don't want our family to be without a roof. We do our best to please our family.

Knowing exactly what you wish for is very different from knowing what it is that you don't want. When you only know what is not in your heart, it's difficult to focus on the good and manifest the worst. Consider this illustration.

Bill doesn't desire to be homeless. He is fed up with living in poverty and wants to be a better person. Bill could follow many different paths to get there. He could become a lawyer, doctor, or other high-paying profession. He might open his own company, invest in real estate, or do other things that could lead to wealth.

Bill is not sure what he would like to do. Bill doesn't know what path will suit him best, so he refuses to choose one.

In his quest to answer this question, the man explores many options. However, once he is faced with hardship, he realizes that it's not the right choice and moves on to another solution.

Bill's actions are not focused. Even though he does work hard, his efforts don't add up. Bill has made twenty little ones, which are much easier to topple than one big impenetrable sand castle. He winds up lost and confused. Bill's failure of focus finally leads to his demise.

What if Bill had decided to follow a particular path? What if he had specific goals in mind? Let's suppose he decides to pursue a career in law. He would know exactly what actions he wanted to take and what he should do.

You will score higher on the LSAT

Get letters from recommendation

Get accepted to the best law school

Select a legal field

Earn a Law Degree

A high-paying job opportunity with a reputable law firm

A specific set of goals is easier to achieve than a vague goal, such as becoming wealthy. Bill has a clear path to follow. Each accomplishment brings Bill closer to the final goal.

Bill's greatest chance of success is likely to be a defined path.

But how will he be able to choose the right path if it isn't what he really wants? Maybe his main goal isn't just to make money. Perhaps he would like to do something he truly loves at the exact same time. Perhaps he is unable to pay for school. Bill isn't willing to make too big of a commitment.

And that is why he falls.

I don't believe this to be a bad thing. Many people are not able to fit neatly onto a particular path. You might find success if you force your way into it, but it's unlikely to make you happy.

This is the important point. If you want to be successful conventionally, you need to choose a route (preferably something mainstream) and work to manifest each step.

Conversely, if you're not concerned about riches or success, you might prefer to spend your time seeking the perfect life.

It is important to not wait too much before making a decision. You lose each moment you take to think.

Chapter 8: Applying The Law Of Attraction

What is visualization and how can it help me? What does visualization mean?

Visualization is the act of creating and using images to convey positive, personal, and powerful messages.

The Dream Board is a visual representation of your dreams.

Use a flat base material, such as cardboard or wooden, to create your own. You also have the option of using a corkboard and tacks. It should be large enough in size to show your goals but small enough to be placed around your home, or at work.

Your ultimate intention is what will guide the materials and methods you use in completing the board. If possible, use one sentence to express your intent.

Example: "I will be done with my university medical program by 2020."

Add images, symbols and objects to your vision board. Ex. Imagine yourself in a doctor's outfit with your name and title MD on it. An image of the hospital that you desire to work at.

You may add numbers that correspond to your target date. Ex: Make a small chart and draw a dream board. This could be when the exam results will finally be available.

Next, put your vision board where it can be seen every day. This will make it easy to meditate on as many times as you want. Your dream board will be more effective if it is placed in a place that has goals. It can be placed in your study or bedroom if it is helping you to prepare for your licensure exam.

Meditation requires you to pay attention to every detail. You must nourish every detail with your faith and energy. It is important to imagine the possibilities for how your dream could become reality. Imagine your goal being achieved. Exist on the dream board. Treat the reality on your dream board like it was your physical reality.

Ex: Imagine yourself in your doctor's uniform. How would you like your clinic to look? Picture yourself as a nurse in a hospital setting, dealing with patients. Feel the atmosphere. Is it bustling? Are you multitasking well? Imagine that you use a therapeutic tone to communicate with your patients.

As with your goals, your dreamboard is not meant as a static thing. Your short-term and long-term goals will change, priorities will shift, or you may need modify elements on your dream boards. This is why you should constantly review your goals.

Affirmations, which can be said to oneself and repeated to another to alter one's thinking patterns, transforming them from negative to positively.

Everyone has a negative voice. We simply listen to that voice and then we act according to it. Affirmations are used to support the positive voice, which can often be muffled by another voice.

It is important to write affirmations in present tense every time you compose them.

I am more effective than you will be.

I am far more efficient than I could wish.

Don't say that I will one day be a physician.

Instead, tell your friends: I am an obstetrician.

The subconscious isn't very effective at distinguishing details.

Therefore, when you say: "I will not procrastinate." Your subconscious automatically picks up that you are both I and Procrastinate

Is this the problem you are seeing?

Let's get this straight:

I'm taking action.

Be a regular user of affirmations to help your brain function. Talk to you in front the mirror each morning and at night. Doing this will allow your conscious psyche to communicate directly with your subconscious.

Another technique is recording your voice and playing the affirmations to yourself in bed. This is how the hypnosis process works. This puts the brain in a relaxed condition, which makes it more susceptible to suggestion.

Visual affirmations can be another option. Assign affirmation signs to your home and hang them all around so you can easily find positive messages while doing your chores.

Mobile phones offer reminders. By setting affirmations that flash on your phone's screen, you can take advantage of the reminders feature. Your screen should flash an affirmation each time your alarm sounds in order to remind of a presentation. Ex.

Stop feeling negative and take a breather. Then, write five minutes of your affirmation. Slowly and meditatively. Believe in every word, every letter. Write your affirmations using your hand. You are transferring energy.

Subliminal message are symbols that have been embedded in another object. They are specifically designed to communicate to the subconscious. It activates an instinctual response within its recipient.

Ex. If you want to lose weight, these messages should appear on your computer screen from time-to-time so that you can view them while browsing or working.

Supermodel!

Get sexy with your salad.

The trick is to keep them coming up again and again. Your brain will be more susceptible to these messages, which will make it more efficient in creating new neural pathways and altering your existing thought patterns.

Keep a journal. A journal may serve various purposes. It can be used to keep track of your progress, make positive lists, and record your successes. It holds together parts of your past as well as the present, so that you have something to go back to in times when you are feeling down. Remembering your past accomplishments will make you realize that you are capable and capable of great things. Writing down gratitude for everything you do every day will show you that your life does not have to be so miserable. A journal that tracks your progress will help you keep track of it and reminds you of the commitment you made. You will see that you can't give up.

The Reality Diary has a unique approach to the standard journal. Instead of simply recording your daily activities, you will be recording your internal reality. The Reality Diary is a way to write as if the reality you live is already yours.

Ex: Today one of my most favorite clients dropped in at the clinic. Although doctors are not supposed to have favorites, I was consulted by her about...

You shouldn't be timid about sharing details in your reality diary. You should enjoy every detail. It's more real inside the more it will appear outside.

Is there a formula that will bring you abundance?

Yes. It's possible. It's:

-Certainty on Vision

-Firmness and Purpose

-Steadiness to Faith

-Depth to Gratitude

The universe will send you a lot of wealth.

This will be a key point to remember when using the law for attraction techniques to attract abundance.

Abundance Checks

Jim Carrey was a popular Hollywood comedian who once wrote himself a check for abundance back in the 90's. This was when he couldn't get any gigs and was flat broke. For his role as an actor, he created a dummy payment dated Thanksgiving 1995 of $10 Million. He believed, along with Oprah Smith and Will Smith in the power of attraction.

Jim was awarded his break. He didn't win it right away, but by 1995, he was making $20,000,000 for each film.

Use a blank or downloaded check to conduct your own abundance check. The more concrete it is, the easier it will be to persuade your subconscious to follow along.

You should write down your full name as well as a specific date. Importantly, note the amount you desire.

This is the time to be realistic. Write down what you are using the money for.

Ex. "As partial compensation for a commissioned picture"

But this only works when you actually paint. Jim set out to obtain a part so he wrote down "for assisting services". Although he was asking for help from all directions, he was still working toward his goal. Think about the reasons why you might receive a paycheck. If you do not own lottery tickets, you won't be able to write it down.

You will then need to sign the check. You may also write Law of Attraction or God or Universe, or whatever name you choose to represent the power that will assist you in achieving abundance.

The abundance check should be treated with respect as it's just like real money. It should be displayed in a prominent place so that you can see it frequently, much like your visualization tools. Jim kept his cash in his wallet.

You can increase your bank account balance

Do this activity in a private, safe area.

Look at your balancebook or online account.

Concentrate only on the numbers. Imagine animated lines moving, expanding, morphing, growing. See more zeros popping up. You can see your balance growing in your mind.

You don't always have to be generous. Sometimes, it pays better to settle and get the amount you need right now. Ex. to pay the bills. Just enough to last until your next paycheck arrives.

Then allow your heart and soul to be filled with genuine gratitude.

The Wealth Bowl

Similar to the Dream Board and the Wealth Bowl, the contents of your wealth container are supposed to visually represent what it is you want. In this case it is wealth.

Place several objects that are symbolic of wealth in a crystal bowl. These objects can be valuable stones, money or jewelry. It doesn't matter if you are using fake gold nuggets of ordinary pebbles painted with gold, they will work just fine.

The bowl should be placed in your home or office.

It's important to remember certain things when you are asking the universe about prosperity.

You have to be grateful that you have any money right now.

Don't waste the money you already have.

Remember that money is also energy so you shouldn't waste it. The one thing that you should know about the energy is that it is infinite. Money, therefore is infinite.

The majority of us were raised with the belief that wealth is a limited resource. Your task is to counter this predetermined belief.

If you believe your parents said that money cannot grow on trees then imagine crisp bills growing from tree branch branches like leaves.

If your current job has taught that money can be difficult to earn, you might see your piles worth of paperwork as a way to turn your paperwork into cash.

Don't say "I can't pay that" or "That's only for wealthy people."

How can I use attraction law to love?

It is important to be open to the possibility for love. It's as easy a smile to the world. A smile is an invitation. A smile conveys love. Every day, start with it. Do you smile at your self in the mirror often? How often are you able to smile at yourself in the mirror? Smile often and openly from your heart. You'll let the universe know you're open to receiving love from all directions.

Empower yourself with love energy. As we have already mentioned, the energy you release will attract. Radiating love energy is the best method to attract energy.

While it might seem hard at the beginning, this is something you should do. It's easy to forget how much you love someone. Do a silent, "I love" to everyone you see, from your boss to your coworkers to your boss to everyone who you meet in the morning and evening.

Chapter 9: Your Personal Blueprint For Breaking The Mold

Now, you have done the mental and emotional heavy lifting mentioned in Chapters 2, 3, and 4. The next step in your journey to freedom is to design a personal blueprint.

This is not a universal solution. All people are different. This is evident. We come from diverse backgrounds, have different experiences, have different expectations.

These differences do add up. These differences are why cookie-cutter solutions that fit all will not work often prove to be a good idea. This is why I expect you adapt the blueprint. Change it. Make it your own. You can change it to fit your unique circumstances or experiences.

Step 1 - Be clear about the triggers

How do you remember past memories? Is it possible to see something that triggers a past memory? Do you often hear certain things? Do past experiences trigger these interpretations in you? These memories may be triggered by specific people.

These triggers can be very different so make sure to know which memories, situations, actions and people you are triggering. Write it down.

Clearly define the connection. Define exactly what the memories are. It is possible that certain situations may trigger particular memories.

Some people might say certain phrases at certain times. This can trigger other memories. It is important to fully map all of this. Be as clear as possible.

Step 2: Start to prepare your mental script

Lack of preparation is usually the reason you have trouble with the past. Some memories trigger negative thoughts, which you know.

It's a well-known fact that when people say certain things to you, it makes you feel terrible. This situation can be very frustrating because it repeats itself over and again and you are not prepared.

You're likely to react in an unacceptable way. You feel humiliated and powerless, ugly, incapable, etc.

This time, you will mix it up. This time, you will map out triggers and determine where they originate. Also, you'll learn which memories trigger what and how you usually react.

This time, however you will try to counteract the interpretations you get from being triggered. You'll prepare a mentally written script.

So, for example, your brother may say to you, "Well at least I didn't drop from college," but you also know that the topic of this matter is brought up in many ways when you talk with him. It causes you to react in a negative manner.

This happens all the time. You can expect it to happen again. Try to interpret the trigger in a way that is more motivating.

Instead of being embarrassed at dropping out of college and then lashing back at your brother/relative, admit it was a mistake. However, acknowledge that you have lived a pretty good life even though college was dropped.

It won't go away. It isn't something you deny. You aren't lying. Instead, look at your successes. Don't dwell on past events.

If you could do this, you'd be powerful. You would stop feeling small. You would be able feel proud and not oppressed.

Instead of constantly focusing on the mistakes in your past, instead look at the victories. You can change from feeling weak to feeling strong.

If you keep doing this, you can go from victim to victor. Victory is something you can choose. It is achievable through your commitment. You take action to get it.

Step #3: Practice makes perfect

Now that you have mapped your triggers out, the next step is to become more proactive. Engage your past memories.

Spend your time talking about painful memories with your closest friend. Engage them.

Engaging past memories is not a waiting game. They will come to you when you trigger them. This is when you can be vulnerable.

These are the times when you are most likely say the incorrect things to the right people at the inappropriate time. This can result in the worst possible results. Instead, it's just you and your friends relaxing at a bar or beach.

Everything is calm. These are the best circumstances to engage with past toxic memories. These are the times when you have most control.

Describe the events. Track your feelings while you are describing the incident. Analyze how you typically react to things. This should be either you or your partner.

Whatever the case may seem, be open about your feelings. Be clear about your typical reactions. Be clear about the triggers.

Then, ask yourself these questions: "How do I act more positively? Or how can I react more neutrally?" Keep thinking of scenarios.

Next, pay attention to the past memory. It will be destroyed. It will be awful, but keep at it. Continue working until you feel positive.

This will not happen overnight. However, practice is the best way to improve.

Step #4: Set an ideal standard of living for yourself

To complete this step, you will need to identify the type of person that you wish to be. This person should not be burdened with mental or emotional baggage.

This is the ideal you. It includes your past and emotions. Be clear about the response of this person. This person should be described in detail. Write down your memories and the responses you would expect from this person.

You should be as specific as possible when describing how your ideal person would respond in different situations or to toxic people. You should clearly define the response of this person.

Keep writing, rewriting and revising the response until you've memorized it. It must be clear, concise and easy to remember. It should be so simple that you have it with you wherever and whenever you need it.

It is important to set a goal to reach this ideal standard. You must understand that it will take time, effort, consistency, and continuous effort to achieve this ideal standard. This is an important commitment.

This is not a thing you do because there are no other things to do. This is not something you do together from time to other.

This is how it works. It is essential to begin it and stay with it. You don't have to give your whole day to it.

You can manage to spend 15 minutes each day. Whatever your case, make sure you give it the attention it deserves.

Step #5: Practice affirmations

After you have established an ideal standard for yourself in emotional reactions, start practicing affirmations. Reaffirm to yourself that you are in control over your life. I take control of my past.

My past doesn't define me. I control the way I interpret and respond. I accept facts the way they are. My past hurts will only help me to be stronger.

Make your own version. They should all lead you to the same place: clarity and strength.

Step #6. Identify and recall the "safe inner place".

Everyone has at minimum one very positive memory. I want to help you find that happy memory. Maybe you have a happy memory from a time when everything was going according to plan.

You felt at peace. There was no one to impress. There was nothing to worry about. Everything was great.

It took place in a specific location and at a specific time. You can see particular details. You can see certain details. Although there are some sounds that you can hear, they all create an inner peace, tranquility, and serenity.

I want to help you recognize that memory and make it your own. This is your mental home. Be aware of your safe inner sanctuary whenever you feel anxious or stressed.

Simply put, this means that you're going replace negative past memories with positive ones. This is how you can tap into the emotional state if calm, power or possibility. You need to give it a command.

Do not forget that this is not a way to get rid of negative memories. No. This will be done after you've called the negative memory out.

You are thinking to yourself, "I am too reading into this positive memory." This memory is based on an imperfect recollection. Are you exaggerating, or are you just reacting in the most negative way to facts?

Whatever the situation, there must be a statement that you own the property. This will ensure that you know what your doing.

You are not denying. It's not enough to just push out negative memories and replace them with happy feelings. If you do this, you are only escaping. This will not help you.

Instead, tell yourself exactly what you're doing. You should tell yourself, "This was what happened with that past memory." I can see the problem.

Chapter 10: A Specialization In Knowledge

There is no universal definition of knowledge. Why not? Because knowledge can be of many kinds. What if you meet something that is "book-smart", but not necessarily "street-smart?" Or vice versa? You may have met someone who could recall the details of a biomechanical device used during a specific exercise and could not identify themselves when they introduced themselves to others at a party. Are you familiar with someone who possesses all of the social gravitas but cannot distinguish between A/C/D currents?

Perhaps someone you knew was highly skilled in a particular area and could explain everything about a computer network's inner workings, but not much else. Another possibility is that you met someone who had a good knowledge of all things but was not an expert in any one topic.

The reason is that there is general knowledge as well as specialized knowledge. Although general knowledge is vast and may be very large, it is possible to have extensive knowledge. However, no matter how much you know it won't help you make more money. A small amount of information won't allow you to excel in one area or have great success in another.

This refers to the requirements of entry-level employees versus those of CEOs in the workplace. General knowledge is enough to get an entry-level job. For CEOs, however you need specialized information. The same holds true for obtaining an education degree. Many bachelor's programmes require a series or classes called "general education," which are exactly what they name: general. These classes provide you with a broad range of knowledge. After your general education, you will then devote the remainder of your studies to specialized classes that are related to your degree. This is where your specialized knowledge comes in handy. It can also help you to be creative.

If knowledge isn't organized and applied, it will not help to save or make money. A plan of action is essential to help you accumulate wealth. People often believe that knowledge is the key to success. However, if knowledge isn't applied to a specific plan and organized properly, it won't result in the money you desire.

Knowledge is only as powerful as the ability to use it. Many educational programs fail you to teach you how organization and use your knowledge.

If you take education to its Latin roots, it means to develop from within. A person who is educated has developed from within. They have developed their mind in order to get what they want. Before you can turn your desires for success or money into reality you will need to be proficient in the area of work or service where you plan to work.

A specialization in knowledge is one of your best assets.

The best thing is that with the internet, and all its related resources you can gain specialized knowledge for almost nothing. The first step in acquiring the specialized knowledge that you require is to identify it. What knowledge are necessary to build websites

Once you have this information, you will be able to turn to the many resources available to help you such as: public libraries; night classes; local community college; and internet classes.

You must organize the information you learn and make use of it through planning. Your knowledge should be applied to achieving your goal. The American modern university system places more importance on degrees that relate to science than to communication or humanities. Science degrees can be applied to specific areas and are useful for specific purposes through practical plans. A generic degree can only be a collection or miscellaneous information that cannot be applied.

You have two options: online classes or in person. First, be sure to know what information you need. Second, ensure that the institution offering it offers it. Reliable sources are important as well. What if you use a Wikipedia page with no verification? Instead, find a trusted and accredited web page, or online notes from a university. But don't stop there.

Successful businessmen are not satisfied with their degrees. They continue to learn and grow as lawyers, doctors, and other professionals . Doctors often attend lectures in their spare hours to continue to learn more. Teachers constantly get recertified, and their current certifications are upgraded to reflect the latest specialized knowledge. Militaries do the same. The most successful people are never satisfied until they have mastered a specific skill. It is impossible to learn website design in one class and expect it be lucrative for years. It is essential to keep learning and improving your skills by taking on more specialized courses.

You can get most of this information from the comforts of your home. You don't need to travel far for a local lecture or certification training group. JavaScript classes are offered at local community colleges so you don't have a need to travel all over the country.

Learning more takes effort. The best things in life are not those that you are given, but those that you work hard for. You can't have it all. The saying "easy comes, easy go" applies to everything. You can tell your child that one toy will cost you, and they will choose a toy they love and play with for a few minutes before getting bored. However, if you give your child an allowance (which they earned through chores around the home), they won't buy the same item twice. They will think hard about how they will spend their money. They worked hard. They worked hard. They are not going to throw it out. Because they worked so hard for it. They will cherish it as a special gift. This is instinctive for all ages. Spending money you don't have is fine if it is not yours. It is time to re-evaluate your spending habits once the money is yours.

Anyone reading this would take a free vacation to an unexplored, deserted area of the planet. It doesn't matter if you have to make the payment for your vacation. You will certainly not visit a country where you don't feel passionate about. You will do all the research and decide on your second favorite location. You'll do all the research required and will be able to learn phrases in the local tongue, so you can enjoy every moment of your vacation.

This all goes back to the old saying "easy comes, easy go". It is difficult for you to appreciate something if you get it easily. However, if you are willing to put in effort to learn it, you'll be more likely to love it. The same applies to learning. Being able to demonstrate self-discipline in acquiring specialized knowledge will increase your appreciation of it. Even if you need to pay for a specialized lecture in a nearby venue, it will help you appreciate the event far more than if all costs were covered.

Many resources are also available online at no cost. Ivy League schools and top universities provide their specialized knowledge free online. This is a fantastic resource that can help you achieve your goals. It is natural for people to consider something more valuable if it comes at a cost. A free education may not be seen as being as beneficial or as valuable as one that costs money. This is exactly why employees require monetary benefits and bonuses to be able to contribute to a company. Employees don't appreciate work if they don't get monetary compensation.

This is something you will need to learn to live with. The value of specialized education does not diminish just because it's free. It is important to take it as seriously as any other education that you would pay for. The same principle is applicable to classes or reading that you do online. A night class at a local college can be a lot easier than an online course. Because you are surrounded and encouraged by others to help you learn, it's much easier than taking an online course. If you miss a lecture, it is an offense to the speaker. It was a waste of their time. It doesn't matter if someone fails to log in to an online class to review the notes. This is another obstacle you'll need to overcome with self-discipline, perseverance and determination if you want success in acquiring the specialized skills you require.

Success is possible by continuously improving your abilities and learning new specialized knowledge. You can find success through many small steps and many different opportunities that come together to create the perfect circumstances. Failure to prepare yourself for all of the opportunities can lead you to failure. If you are prepared and have the specialized knowledge necessary to make a plan for every situation, you can be ready.

Consider Steve Jobs. He also took a calligraphy program during his time in formal school. It did not affect his degree but served as an opportunity to enhance his skills and knowledge. Although he did not see the purpose of taking the course at that time, he knew that it would have some application. He was eventually able, using the skills he had learned in calligraphy, to create the different fonts you see in Apple's programs today. Steven Jobs's calligraphy skills were the basis of the text you are currently reading. He wouldn't have been able to design fonts had he not taken that extra course.

Take a cue from Steve Jobs and learn specialized knowledge.

Chapter 11: New Scientific And Medical Discoveries

If science and medicine were to stop, would mankind continue on? It's unlikely. Creativity should not be restricted to the Arts and Entertainment. Creative thinking is required for every aspect of our culture. This book is incomplete without a chapter about some of the most innovative players in Science, Medicine and Engineering.

Jorge Odon Inventor of Odon Device

Sometimes the most unlikely of solutions lead to the best solutions. Imagine a man with no medical education creating a device to aid childbirth in developing country. Jorge did exactly that. Like most inventions, it began with a problem. In developing countries, 97% of deaths occurring in childbirth occur because of a lack training for doctors and inadequate equipment.

Jorge's next phase was caused by an extremely random issue. Jorge, who was working as an automotive mechanic, saw his coworkers removing the cork from a glass bottle using a plastic container. He learned how to do this from a YouTube YouTube video. Jorge woke up later that night thinking: What if this bottle was a uterus and cork was a baby for childbirth?

Jorge began to put his skills to use and created a glass tube uterus that was filled with one daughter's dolls. He took his idea to Buenes Aires' teaching hospital. It was well received. Jorge and his staff helped him to obtain the patents. Jorge turned 30 on Jorge's Birthday, March 1, 2011. They were all successful. Jorge quit his job in mechanic to work full-time on the Odon device.

Jorge used a random idea to create a device that would solve a totally different problem. This is the result creativity and demonstrates that people can come up with amazing products even if they are not in their field.

Chase Adam, CoFounder/CEO of Watsi

There is always more work in the developing countries. Medicine is one the most important fields that require more people and greater innovation. This is why it's absurd to think that these countries have people who die or receive second-class healthcare. Chase Adam is one example of someone making that less common.

Chase is focused to identify high-benefit, low risk areas where creativity could occur in the medical industry. The subject can be sensitive due to privacy issues and other factors. Chase believes that placing more emphasis on user experience in healthcare will make the industry grow leaps and bounds. While the focus has been on the business aspects of the healthcare industry, there has not been much innovation in the patient side.

So, what can Chase do as a part of making these ideas a reality. Watsi was a platform which allows crowd-funding. It allows users and others to donate directly for medical treatment in developing country. Chase has taken the small piece of this puzzle and put it together to solve the issue of money for those who would otherwise go without proper treatment.

Chase began by solving a very small problem in a limited area. It is clear that Chase is working hard on the next one.

Carl Hart is a Columbia University neuroscientist

Although drug addiction and drug abuse have been a significant problem for some time, are we really as addicted as we think? Carl Hart believes otherwise. In 2012, he conducted and published a study that showed that meth users would prefer to spend $20 on meth than $20 on heroin. Carl has also done research to show that drug addiction can be explained by environment and not brain impulse, which is what most people think.

Carl believes that addiction is being used on a too large scale. He has also spoken out against government representatives. He has taken a stand against scientific inconsistencies as well as policies that often disadvantage the underprivileged. Carl draws from his growing up in a Miami area rough neighborhood to say that scientists tend not to portray drug addicts/drug takers in stark contrast with what he observed growing up.

Carl isn't going to let science trends dictate the science behind his experiences. His research and position on drug abuse research deserve praise.

Kathryn Hunt, Paleo-Oncologist

What if your expedition in Egypt was over and you returned to find out you had ovarian Cancer? Kathryn Hunt had to experience this. In remission, she started putting the pieces together shortly after that expedition. Many bones that she was studying revealed signs of disease. The ancient record mentioned cancer numerous times. Because it was unclear what the ancient records would have looked like, there was little evidence.

Kathryn and a few others founded the Paleo-Oncology Research Organization. In that time, they have found more than 220 cases of likely cancer in ancient societies. This led to them creating an open-source data base for researchers to use in order to exchange and discuss information.

Kathryn hopes that funding will be available to allow her to examine some of those cases in greater detail using radiological analyses and DNA testing. She hopes she will be able identify patterns within the ancient record and offer researchers areas in which to concentrate more closely.

Kathryn, a victim of her own failures, put two and three together and made great strides in the study and treatment of ancient societies.

Chapter 12: Neuro Linguistic Programming For Focus

Neuro Linguistic Programming also known simply as NLP, is a method to use language and neurolinguistic patterns to create new connections between the brain and the body. It can be used to accomplish specific goals and change existing ones. NLP can be seen as a technology because it is focused on "what works", rather than on theories.

This system is based the Noam Chumbsky system of transformational language, which states languages have two levels of representation. NLP assists clients in overcoming their problems.

NLP for Improving focus

NLP techniques to increase focus are often taught in workshops. NLP trainers believe the mind is hard to control. There will be moments when your mind is fully engaged and you are not easily distracted. However, there will also be times when your attention is lost.

NLP sessions will help you identify distractions that keep you from being fully focused and prevent you from doing so. These distractions can be classified into two main categories: External and Internal Distractions.

Internal distractions are thoughts on past and/or future (instead focus on the current moment), negative thoughts, such as self criticism and criticism towards another person, and thoughts that make you anxious or afraid.

External distractions can be noise, visuals, or tactile factors that distract from your ability to focus on the important. These include the temperature, Internet, and people around.

People are idiosyncratic. They respond differently to distractions. NLP teaches how to preserve your mental energy so that you can focus. You can adjust your behaviour to support your ability to concentrate, including sleeping properly, eating healthy food and exercising.

Under the guidance of an NLP coach you will also learn how positive thinking works, how the present can be a force for good, how to cope with the past and how to feel free in the future, as well as how to use NLP to help you become more open to the possibilities.

How to Improve Focus and Apply NLP

You do not need to register for an NLP course if time and money are tight. This is why you can still enjoy NLP using the Trigger Method.

Step 1: Pay attention to your surroundings. Take note of everything you see.

Step 2 Close your eyes. Focus on the emotion that is causing you to lose focus. This can come in the form of joy, frustration, and encouragement. You can use this emotion to increase your power.

Step 3 - Continue building upon the emotional state to expand your mind and become all you think about. Slowly open up your eyes and begin to look at your surroundings.

Step 4: Clear your mind. Step 4: Clear your mind.

Step 5 Continue to go through Steps 2/3.

NLP can help you link the emotions that will cause you to focus with the environment. Make sure you don't do it in a relaxing environment (like your bedroom), but instead in a conducive one (such like your office).

Chapter 13: Visualizations For Love And Romance

For a partner to love you, you have to first love yourself. This is not always easy because many of us are subject to traumas or programming from past relationships and/or childhood.

But it is possible to learn how to love yourself. It is worthwhile and can have a major impact on how you live your life and view the world.

You're sitting comfortably with pink light surrounding you. It feels as though you are being given a hug from someone who cares deeply about you. You can feel the hug from your parent, grandparents, partner or friend. This person will not let go of you unless or until you give it some signal. You can be held in their arms for as many hours as you wish. You feel loved, secure, warm and safe.

Chance Meeting

You're in your favorite café, restaurant, or some other place that you enjoy, and you are looking for a quiet spot where you can just sit down. A man or woman approaches you, looks directly in your eyes, and asks if they can join you.

Normally, you would laugh at such behavior. But it's almost like the person is sent to you.

You feel a spark and like you like what you've seen, so you agree and invite him/her to join you at the table.

You have a great conversation. It feels like you are in a relationship. You arrange for a second meet-up. You feel great, like you're in high school again and have been asked to go to prom by the girl/guy that you want.

Secret Admirer

You are in a place where drinks will be served, such as at a coffee shop. Place your order, and you sit down to wait for the beverage. When your drink is ready, you reach for your wallet but the bartender/waitress/barista says, "It's on that guy/girl over there." You look across the room and the person who bought your drink looks directly at you and nods. You like the things you see. You want to show your appreciation. Soon you will find yourself talking to each other like old friends.

Hurtbox

Your body is relaxed on a mattress and about to fall asleep. Two people can enter the room, one of which is you. The wall behind your eyes opens to reveal the conveyor belt. The machine is switched on and the belt moves, but it's barely acoustic. One of them asks if you're ready. You begin to think about all the sad and painful times you have experienced. Each thought is taken, placed on the belt, then travels through a machine until it reaches large boxes and is finally dumped in there. You begin to think. Each thought is taken and placed on the conveyor. They seem like they'll never end but eventually, they slow down. Soon you are free from all your unhappiness and regrets, and you agree that the session should be ended. The box is sealed once all of your unhappy memories, regrets and trauma have been removed. When you are asked if it would be okay to look at the box one more time, you say no. The contents of this box, along with the unhappy contents, are put in an incinerator where they can be turned into ash.

The Power Within

Many of us have heard about the "subconscious" mind. We all have it. However, we don't know exactly what it is, how it functions, or how we can master its secrets. The subconscious mind doesn't exist. It is an integral part you. It's almost like a supercomputer. It exists to help you create the life you want.

Your subconscious has been programmed from the moment you were born and likely even before. Your subconscious has been shaped (in both good and bad ways) by your parents and teachers. Others, like your romantic partners, friends, coworkers, and even colleagues later on in life have had an impact in shaping events and experiences that are based on thoughts, habits, or beliefs. We are all creatures of habit. Your thoughts are, in a certain sense, habits. Every day you have the exact same thoughts or patterns of thinking.

This "thinking" can be shaped by repetition. A habit is an action sequence, such as the steps required to make a sandwich. This can be repeated every day or almost every single day. As it is with thoughts. Virtually every person has recurring habits of thoughts. These thoughts can have an impact on how we see the world and ourselves.

These thoughts can be whatever you think. They are combined with advice from parents and other important people to help you navigate the world.

The subconscious mind doesn't think creatively. This is not its job. It cannot differentiate between what is imaginary' and what it is real'.

The "operating system" is a set of thoughts and visual images that you repeatedly repeat and keep in your mind. It stores, organizes, interprets the data you have accumulated from your pre-dominant thoughts. It helps you attract or create the circumstances you want.

It's pretty impressive when you think about!

Our conscious brain acts as a programmer. It's also the creative mind, the thinking brain. However, you can influence the subconscious with filters that your dominant thoughts have stored and created. The subconscious mind, like a computer program, doesn't judge or discriminate what can be achieved. The conscious mind is able to evaluate a situation, decide what is right and incorrect, and then it imprints this information in the subconscious.

"Failure Programs" refer to negative habits, thoughts, and beliefs that are imprinted within the subconscious mind. They include thought habits such as saying you can't do it, won't get something, don't deserve anything, etc. These negative habits become part and parcel of your subconscious. This decreases inner confidence, and results in capability suppression.

This can create a vicious cycle.

If you master the conscious mind and infuse the right programming into your subconscious, you will be unstoppable. This will give you more control over your subconscious mind's incredible abilities to make you aware and take action. When you harness the power within your subconscious mind, you can manifest everything you desire.

Beginnings of mastery

Understanding your inner speech will give you the information that you need to master you mind.

Realizing how powerful you are at manifesting your life's circumstances can be both challenging and rewarding. The subconscious mind is a machine that works by habit. By imprinting positive, optimistic, "can-do" thoughts over and above the old ones, you can replace them with newer habits. To replace old habits, create neural pathways based in positive "I Can Be/Do/Have Thinking".

Change begins with you

in. You can make changes in your life, such as changing jobs, ending relationships, moving, and so on. You can move, change jobs or end relationships. But, unless your "change of mind" is from within, it will be difficult to attract more people like you. It will continue to be "same stuff" with different people, locations, and jobs.

Meditation is one of the best ways to connect with yourself and the images in your mind. You can transform the way you live your life by engaging in daily visualizations. You might be shocked at how many thoughts and beliefs you hold that can keep you from achieving what you want. It is possible to imprint the most positive programming through routine practice.

When you do this, you'll start to notice synchronicity everywhere.

It won't require much. Just by paying more attention to your thoughts and spending some time visualizing positive outcomes, you can start to notice the difference. You may notice some amazing and unusual things.

You will find the right person for you at the perfect time. You might find the right person to help you. You may also be in a bookstore or library when you find the right book. Perhaps a stranger might buy your cup of coffee.

When your outer world is a mirror to the new amazingness you find in your inner life, it makes life incredible fun.

Visualization has existed since humankind first inhabited the earth. Images have been used in therapeutic applications by many ancient civilizations. These include the Navajos and ancient Egyptians. Judaism as well as Hinduism have practiced imagery (or what we call visualization). "Guided imagery" is a term that can be used to describe many techniques including metaphor, storytelling (fantasy), game playing, dream interpretations drawing, visualization and active imagination.

Visualization, which can be done either through reading, audio, or by your own imagination, can help you relax, and allow you to focus on images that are related to personal issues. Experiential guided imagery practitioners may employ an interactive, objective guiding style. This allows them to solve problems by exploring their own inner resources. Biofeedback may be used in combination with imagery to aid in meditative relaxation. You can access interactive guided imagery classes, workshops, classes, seminars, audio tapes, books, and audio cassettes.

You will be able to visualize as long as there is a quiet area and your own mind.

Remember These Things

Laying the Foundation

Your thoughts, words and actions have incredible power.

Most people know that thoughts and words can be spoken, but thoughts cannot be spoken. You can alter the way you think, speak and act to create your reality. The best way to do that is to take a look at yourself before you make a negative comment or think about it. How many times were you irritated by something someone said to you? It wouldn't bother you if they never said it or you hadn't heard it. Consider what it would be like if you had an idea and suddenly felt upset.

It does not matter whether you or another person say something mean or hurtful.

Sometimes our inner dialogue towards ourselves can be hurtful and negative. This is only one example of how powerful thoughts or words can be and how they impact us.

Keep that in mind. It's important to realize that any negative thoughts or actions you have are continuing to programme your subconscious. It doesn't make a difference if it is towards yourself or others.

If you tell yourselves that you can't accomplish something (that your heart desires), such as writing a poem or fixing something, you are setting you up for failure. How many times in your lifetime have you done it? You probably have. This is the stuff we live with every day.

You can reduce your vibration by thinking or talking negatively if you do so regularly. It can be a sort of domino effect.

I didn't excel at this so I won't try it. You not only put yourself at risk of failure, but you also expect failure to be automatic and certain. This can lead to you giving up on trying and failing. How can you be sure it won't turn out? This kind of thinking for a lifetime can lead to endless amounts of lost dreams and hopes.

It is truly sad to see so many people living like this. However, millions of people are forced to deal with it every day.

On the flipside, you can say what if and why not. That's where there is magic. Let's say, for example that you were interested in taking a dance class. You could choose to try a different form of dancing, or you might enjoy any new activity. You'd likely find others who are new to the class. Even if those weren't the case, that doesn't mean they aren't worth it. You have got to start somewhere. And learning can be fun. Although it sounds cliché, you can't really know if you don't give up. The saddest thing is to look back on your past with regret at not having tried the thing/things - fill in blank — that you had always wanted to try but never did.

KEEP YOUR "FILTER CLEAN."

Aside from being mindful of what your words and thoughts are, there are several things you can do to improve the effectiveness of visualizations. It won't happen overnight but you will start to see improvement with regular practice.

This basically involves getting rid of all negativity. It is impossible to protect yourself completely but you can minimize the negative energy that comes into your mind.

One solution is to not watch the news or read the newspaper. There is so much negativity in the news, and even media. It's a daily avalanche, and it's something you can do little about. A suggestion: If the news is something you cannot miss, consider watching some of it from one or more of the shows like Last Week Tonight.

Another way to avoid or limit negative contact is to avoid them. Some people thrive on negativity, and they want to lure others into their misery. You are likely to know at most one person like this. Even though you may feel that you are hurting them or being antisocial when you decline their invitation to dinner, they will soon find someone else. You'll feel a lot better.

You should also avoid gossiping. It may be difficult, but gossiping could be the sister of misery mashing. While it sounds cheesy at first, you wouldn't want anyone gossiping about you. People who gossip around you and with you are likely to be gossiping about your absence. You will be a better human being if you don't gossip. This might be the foundation for better visualization. Consider this if your belief in karma (repaying what you sow) is important.

You don't have the right to strive for sainthood or perfection. But you can work towards improvement. Any improvement is better than none. Positively think about how you feel every time something goes your way.

Besides this, ... is another option.

TRY NOT to COMPLAIN TOO MUCH

Complaining does not do anything other than to create negativity and keep it alive. There are times when it is okay to complain, but only if the issue needs to be fixed. If you're dining at a restaurant and the food is cold, it would be a good idea to make a complaint. If you complain about every single thing, or a lot of things during the day it can have a domino impact on your life and create more reasons to be unhappy. Negative experiences are more likely to occur in your life if you do not complain about the little stuff.

Chapter 14: Become Happier By Conditioned Stimuli

To realize and experience what you want in this life, you need to raise your vibration. It is possible to increase your wellbeing level and your happiness. However, there will be times when you don't feel well or your happiness dips. This happens sometimes all at once. What can be done in such moments? You can condense a stimulus in a way that makes you feel happy and positive in a matter of seconds. Then, use it whenever you want.

Pawlow (a Russian scientist) has proven that conditioned stimuli can function. Pawlow also experimented using dogs. Similar experiments were made with dogs and other living species.

It should also be noted that conditioned stimuli do not create habits. A stimulus is the stimulus that triggers a reaction. We are taught to answer the phones when they ring. The ringing is the stimulus and answering is what happens.

I was in pain for several years before I found relief. No pain-killing pills were strong enough. I discovered that the brain sets pain. You don't have to feel the pain if you have a reason.

Pawlow's experiments in dogs was fascinating to me. He would hit a bell at a time each day. This was just a few minutes after they had eaten. After about three weeks, they were able to hit the gong well before their mealtime. Dogs arrived looking hungry. The dogs didn't seem hungry. They were used to eating after the gong was heard.

A conditioned stimulus may also help with pain, which I correctly predicted. I believed that happiness and joy make it easier to forget about pain. I decided to create a stimulus for happiness, wellbeing, and health. I chose a stimulus. Next, I thought about times in my past that made me happy. Finally, I put my happiness stimulus into action. For the next three weeks, I repeated this process several times per day. Finally, I tested my happiness stimuli. I pushed the stimulus until the pain was severe. It worked for a brief time. The brain structure changes were explained at the beginning. There are two options for strengthening or decreasing the brain structure. You have to repeat this over several weeks, months, and then you can either strengthen or decrease your synapses. I used my happiness stimulus when the pain was intense. I assumed that I had to continue using the happiness and wellbeing stimuli until the pain part in my brain receded. The pain began to diminish in strength. It took almost three years to get rid of the pain.

Although three years seems like a long amount of time, how do you compare to years of pain? It depends on what kind of personality you have and how much you wish to rid yourself of it. If you are an angry person, it will depend on how old and deep the characteristic is in your brain. You will stop feeling anger when you use happiness stimulation. It might take a while if you're young. As you age, it will take more time.

There are many ways to use the happiness stimulus. You can use it against sudden anger or being frightened. It can also be used against depressing situations, such as when you need self esteem.

I concluded that one can increase his wellbeing and happiness as well as raise the emotional frequency of vibration. This will lead to a better lifestyle.

Understanding the importance of conditioning a stimulus can help you to increase happiness and well-being.

Condition a Stimulus for a Happier You.

Choose a stimulus. It should be a pressing action that is discreet. You can press one finger into another by pressing. It is best to press with one hand on the other. Consider a stimulus that you can use in a way that is not noticeable even if someone is watching.

Give it the name Happiness Stimulus and condition it to promote happiness and wellbeing.

How to induce happiness

a. When you feel happy, press your happiness stimulation.

b. Relax, close your eyes, open your eyes, and picture a very happy moment. You can either imagine it or recall something.

This can be done several times daily for at minimum three weeks to condition your Happiness Stimulus. You need to condition it.

After your Happiness Stimulus becomes conditioned, you are able to use it whenever required.

When you feel unhappy or sad, activate your happiness stimulus. You will experience a surge of happiness and well-being. For those who feel angry or sad, activate your happiness stimulus to bring joy and stop the sadness.

It is important to remember that happiness equals painlessness. Your happiness stimulus must also work against pain.

You can condition a stimulus to produce any characteristic or emotion. It is important to limit the number or frequency of stimuli you are able to condition. It is better to limit your options to just three stimuli. You can make one more self-assured, which might be helpful if you are extremely insecure. For students, you could also condition the stimulus to be focused. The Happiness Stimulus can be the most important stimulus. The Happiness Stimulus is the most important stimulus. It makes you happy and helps you achieve your goals. Happiness should be your first priority.

WHY SHOULD WE VISUALIZE CONSCIOUSLY?

Your subconscious and uncontrolled visualizing is what keeps you awake at night. Your life goals are clear. You are able to focus your attention on your goals.

We don't perceive what we see. What we perceive will depend on the patterns in neural activity that is going on within our brains. Science Daily 2007 Nov 20: This information was taken from Science Daily 2007. In other words, we see with the brain. The brain controls the hardware. Software is thought, feelings, and the programming of the subconscious are the hardware. What you put into the system is what you hear, see and feel. You upload software to your system by visualizing one of your wishes repeatedly. This will change the wiring in your brain.

Our thoughts are pictures. Though you can say that they are turned into pictures, it does not mean that the thought itself is transformed into a picture. Our thoughts are converted into pictures. It is the frequency at which our perceptions are influenced by these feelings that we generate vibrations. The creative visualization of images can help you change your thoughts and create a new way of seeing them.

When you think of dinner you don't necessarily see the term "dinner". Instead, you may see certain foods on the table or held in one's hands. Peter isn't a name you hear. Instead you see Peter as the person you are. If you have debts, you might be afraid to get into that position. This image of you street-begging might not occur to you. You may see it as reality if your thoughts are often focused on debt. Instead of thinking about debt, celebrate the fact that your bank accounts are positive.

As you can see, thoughts (or pictures) are not only conscious but also unconscious. This is why controlling your thoughts, emotions and thoughts is crucial. It is possible to reprogram your thoughts to only think positive thoughts unconsciously and consciously. Be positive in your thinking, visualize what you want, stay positive and happy. Your unconscious thoughts will then be positive.

It is known that your mind will focus on a specific object if you keep it focused for a time. It is essential that you control what you think and how you perceive the world, both in real life and in your imagination. Imagines have a tremendous impact.

After having thought about what words you would use, you start to speak. You speak only after you have thought of what you will say. Thinking and feeling are activated by the things you see, hear or smell. You can see that everything around you has an influence on your thinking. Many of those thoughts are subconscious. If your feelings suddenly change, unconscious thoughts might start to surface.

If you've ever met someone who nags or talks endlessly about their problems, you know how it affects your mood. This can make your entire day miserable and lead to further problems. You must get out of the path of such people!

It's a good thing to have a cookie when you're stressed and don't feel great. These childhood memories might not be something you are aware of, but it will change the way you feel. It can change how you live your life.

Your frequency of vibration drops when you watch bad news on TV. This will make you feel worse. Your next thought will probably be negative, and without you being aware, you'll find yourself in a depressed state. The next bad thought is followed by a negative emotion. This vicious circle can result in more bad thoughts. Even though things don't go according to plan, it is possible to ask yourself how you got there.

I stated it earlier and I continue to repeat it often: You need to choose carefully what you watch, listen, look at, and read. It is also important to consider where you live, what clothes you wear, and how your home and furniture are made. The quality of your life and wellbeing will depend on the people you interact with.

What can you do if there's no way to get out of something negative? Do something you enjoy, as soon as you can. Find inspiration from your feeling-good-list to help you choose something that will make it feel better. Turn on the radio and find some music to cheer you up. Enjoy a meal, even if dinner is coming up. Contact a friend, or someone you care about who is positive. Go for a run, swim, or just to relax. Go on a walk through a park or to the countryside to take in the beautiful scenery. It is important to not return to your old routine after a bad experience. Instead, find something positive and replace it with something better.

Pictures = Thoughts = Feelings = Emotional Frequency Vibration = Perception

Thoughts are feelings

Pictures are thought (pictures) and then converted into feelings. Thoughts, feelings, and thoughts are all interconnected. They correlate to 100 percent. Let me clarify that thoughts are feelings.

This means your thoughts should be positive when you feel good. If you feel bad, your thoughts are negative. Depressed people see the world around them in dark colors. They focus on the problems. When you feel happy, all around you is bright. You are aware of all the wonderful possibilities and everything you do works out well.

If you want to live a happier, healthier life, feeling good is key. Make sure you're aware of your emotions and take steps to make it better. Pay attention to your thoughts and take control!

Frequency and intensity of vibration = how you feel

Your thoughts (pictures + feelings) produce a certain frequency that vibrates, which is responsible f what you perceive.

Your thoughts about the past years will influence what you see and do.

The way you perceive things will depend on what you think about them and how you feel right now.

With your thoughts, your feelings can shape your tomorrow.

Visualize scenes and scenes in bright colors. You will experience a more positive outlook and a more fulfilled life. It is essential to feel right now what you will feel later.

Frequency and Perception of Vibration

Your dream is to live in a mansion and have employees. Yet, it's not possible. Your frequency of vibratory is low, so you are unable to perceive the rewards for all that you have done. You must be active. However it isn't about how hard your work but how you feel.

This is the 3rd lesson. I have previously written about how your feelings matter and why it is so important. It was the main focus of lesson 2a and 2b. You can feel a lot better if you tell me that you feel good. And this is crucial.

Your life will begin to change if your happiness and wellbeing are increased. This will not happen in a single direction, but it will definitely be an improvement. This happens because your perception is affected by how happy or well you feel. Take lesson 2a & 2b very seriously if you haven't read them.

The truth is that you can transform your life dramatically by changing what you think about and how you feel. This can be controlled by images which you consciously visualise repeatedly. The faster you feel good and more positive, the easier it will be to succeed in all aspects.

You visualize or call it picturing. Creative visualization is when you see images and scenes of what your heart desires.

Chapter 15: The Seven Universal Laws

The Seven Universal Laws (or principles) govern everything in this Universe. These laws allow the Universe to exist in perfect harmony. The Universe dates back over 5,000 year ago. This could be traced back ancient mystical, esoteric as well as secret teachings. These came from Ancient Greece through Egypt, as well as the Vedic tradition of Ancient India. They all have the connecting threads the seven spiritual law of the Universe. Transform your life in many ways once you learn, align and practice these Universal Laws.

Universal Laws Mutable and Inimmutable. These three eternal laws are indestructible, meaning they can't be changed. They will remain in existence forever. These four laws are temporary and can be transcended to make your ideal reality. These laws are essential to your existence and should not be ignored. To master each of these Universal laws, you will need to be able to master the others.

1) The Law of Mentalism. This is the first Universal Law. It tells us that all of the universe's laws are mental. It states all that we can see and feel in our physical world was created within the invisible mental realm. It states that the Universe is made up of one consciousness-the Universal Mind-from which all things can be created. The Universal Mind is the subordinate of all things created at various levels. Your mind, which is a part in the Universal Mind, is the same as the Universal Mind. However, the only difference is one degree. Your reality is in fact a manifestation of you mind.

2) The Law of Correspondence. The second Universal Law states that there is harmony and correspondence between the mental, physical and spiritual realms.

Everything in the Universe derives its energy from one source. There is no separation. This pattern also applies to all planes of existence, starting with the largest star up to the smallest of electrons. All is one. In an inscribed, the Ancient Greek Temple Apollo from Delphi mentioned the law of correspondence. It said, "Know yourself and you will be able to know all the secrets of the gods.

3) The Law of Vibration. The third Universal law is that everything vibrates, moves and rests according to the seventh. It states that the entire Universe is a vibrating system. Science has established that all energy vibrating at different frequencies in the Universe is pure energy. The Law of Attraction was founded on the law of "like energy attracts like". Vibrations drive everything we experience in this physical realm. This applies also to the mental realm. Your thoughts can be described as vibrations. Your emotions are vibrations too. The highest level of emotional vibration is that which represents unconditional love. The power of thought can be used to alter your mental vibration.

4) The Law of Polarity. The fourth Universal Law states that there can be no one but two opposites. It is the first mutable law. It means there are two sides. This holds true for good, evil, light, dark, positive, neutral, war, peace,

love, and hate. You can consciously alter your vibrations by changing your hatred to love or fear towards courage. This is called Polarization in the ancient Hermetic Traditions.

5) The Law of Rhythm. The fifth Universal Law tells us all things have highs or lows. Everything has its tides. It is the second universal law.

6) Laws of Cause and Effect. The sixth Universal law teaches us that every cause has its effect and all effects have their cause.

Every effect you perceive in your world physical has a cause in our mental world. First, master your mind to be in control of your destiny. Everything that is in your world was created by your subconscious mind.

7) The Law Gender. The last of the seven Universal rules states that gender is in all things, and that all things have their feminine and male principles.

Chapter 16: Sunflower Visualization

Allow your body time to relax. Your arms, hands and legs can rest on the sides of your body or on top of your heart chakra. Be sure to wear comfortable clothes, but not too tight.

Close your eyes. Allow yourself to be present. Do not allow your thoughts to enter your head. If you have any, let them in and they will roll away as waves that gently approach the lakeshore.

Waves slowly move in and out, one by one. Every thought should be in tune with the tides. Every emotion should go inward and outward.

Enjoy the moments of relaxation and take your time. You have complete control over your time and space. There is nothing you need to do at this time. You do not have to do anything at this moment.

While your mind might wander to other thoughts, focus on the present experience.

Breathe deeply. Breathe positive energy. Breathe out love energy. Inhale negative energy, and exhale anger. Do this three to 5 times in succession.

It is a safe place where you can feel comfortable and at ease. You are now safe from harm and can feel secure. You can only access this place because it is yours.

Do not hold onto any preconceived notions about what you should be doing. Accept yourself as you are. Allow the experience itself to flow naturally. Breathe at the pace that is most comfortable for you.

You can take in the golden sunlight while you are walking through the rows and row of sunflowers. Take a moment to look up at the long stems. Feel the golden sun's light travel down to surround you and illuminate all of your activities.

You feel comfortable in the summer light, which captures your inner beauty. Feel great as you swirl around in the summer light and feel the peace that radiates through.

You are confident in your own abilities and character. Others' opinions may not reflect the real nature of your character. You are unique, real, and authentic. Be gentle and understanding of yourself.

Your self-worth doesn't depend on anyone else. You are becoming an attractive flower. Petal by petal, you're becoming taller like a strong sunflower.

Lift your head towards the sky, and let the sun radiate sunshine into your heart. All the emotions and feelings you have that make other people feel unworthy of you must be wiped away. You have the power and freedom to feel happy and free.

As you stare at a reflection, sparkles of sunshine twinkle on the glass of the river. You are a marvellous creation. You were created by God. Perfect in every way, perfect through his unconditional love.

You do not have to feel ashamed or guilty of who you really are. Allow the sun to shine upon whatever is not serving your highest good.

Allow yourself to shine inwardly as brightly as the shining sun.

Believe in yourself and don't be afraid to try your best. Accept yourself as the person you are. Recognize all the wonderful things about you that make God's love complete.

Begin to run through the fields full of sunflowers. Be open to the feeling of love. Recognize that it's fine to be you, no matter what others think.

You can enjoy the sunshine and the tender warmth of a young soul that believes in itself. The world is full with possibilities and nothing is impossible.

Be able to feel the softness within every silk flower. The flower's inner beauty resonates with your nakedness. You are precious, fragile and you should be loved.

God gave you the freedom to be yourself without regrets. You can shine like the golden sun wherever you go.

Sending love and support to yourself as you travel along the back roads all the way back home. Have gratitude for who your are.

You can take a moment to just breathe and be silent as you realize how beautiful you are.

Listen to water rush forward in water, water will do its best to move with the current downstream.

The saltiness of sunflower seeds will cleanse your palate.

The sunflowers will touch the tip your nose. Take a few of them and bend over to see them reaching for the sun.

Breathe the fresh air in and let go any negative energy. Take in the love that cleans your soul.

The breeze will gently sweep your rosy cheeks. Relax and allow yourself to be still.

As long as you'd like, keep this feeling. You can stop this meditation at any time.

You can simply open your eyes. For a few moments, relax, and let your body adjust to the meditation.

Couple's Visualization

Relax. Your arms, hands and legs can rest on the sides of your body or on top of your heart chakra. Be sure to wear comfortable clothes, but not too tight.

Close your eyes. Allow yourself to be present. Do not allow your thoughts to enter your head. If you have any, let them in and they will roll away as waves that gently approach the lakeshore.

Waves slowly move in and out, one by one. Every thought should be in tune with the tides. Every emotion should go in and out, forward and zurück.

Enjoy the moments of relaxation and take your time. You have complete control over your time and space. At this particular moment, there is no one else to be. There is nothing that you need to do at this time.

While your mind may drift to other thoughts, focus on the present experience.

Breathe deeply. Breathe positive energy. Breathe out love energy. Breathe in the love energy. Do this three- to five times a day.

It is a safe place where you can feel comfortable and at ease. You are now safe from harm and can feel secure. You can only access this place because it is yours.

Do not hold onto any preconceived notions about what you should be doing. Accept yourself as you are. Allow the experience of being there to flow naturally. Allow your body to relax at its own pace.

Allow the light of the emerald green to illuminate your heart chakra. You will feel the love of the angels filling the room with their unconditional love. Enjoy the pure white light from the angels and feel their warmth surrounding you.

For the love of your life, open your heart and feel it. Take a walk through the green forest. You can feel the sunlight filtering through the trees as you walk along the path. Explore the diverse shapes of the ferns, and fauna.

Breathe deeply and enjoy the freshness of each step. Notice the texture of the moss as you gaze over the ground. Some are flat while others are star-shaped. Notice how mushrooms sprout everywhere. Green fills the forest in nature's love.

Every stem of every flower, every leaf, each blade of grass and moss is a part of nature. Nature's unconditional love embraces you, and keeps your feet steady.

Surrounding the mountain cliff is the beautiful view of large amounts of water. The sun's light reflects off the water and brightens your eyes as you stare at the westhorizon. The water here is calm and still.

You see your partner as you turn. As you reach out and hug each other, you feel his love. You kiss each other on both of your cheeks. Smiles radiate across the faces of each other. You invite one another into each others' lives.

Both of your feelings are safe with each other. Both of your trust in one another. Both of your faith is in each other. There is nothing between you. You will be loyal to each other.

Every negative thought that floats through your mind is fear. Accept it. It was there to remind your heart and partner how fragile it is right now.

Keep in mind that pure unconditional Love is free from fear. Love and fear cannot coexist. Pure love, which is all there really is, is the best thing.

Archangel Michael may help you to let go all of your worry, anxiety, or fear. Ask him if he can fill your heart up with the graces and love.

Know that you are safe with the person who you love and that they will stay in your life if you have your best interests at heart.

There's no need to worry about losing your partner. Even if they have to leave at some point, you've had the chance to share in the love of your life with them. God's love is unbreakable.

Thanks to your partner for the many lessons and gifts you receive every day. Thank them for showing you the real you. We are grateful for their ability to show us that love is real.

Forgive and forget about the pain and anger that they have caused. Forgive your partner for not being a perfect person in your own life. Forgive them if you are not perfect in your own life.

Accept that you're both learning and changing over time. You are both perfect, in spite of your imperfections.

Partner, exchange pink flowers. Ask them to live with peace and unity. You can help them be their best. Be your best self. Enjoy harmony and peace together until the forest edge.

Give them a hug and a kiss on their cheeks. Turn and walk back along the forest. It is a great feeling to have had the opportunity to reflect on your unreserved love for your partner. They have shown you love and appreciation.

As long as you'd like, keep this feeling. When you're ready, you can stop this meditation at any time.

You can simply open your eyes. For a few seconds, relax and let your body adjust back to its normal state.

Deep Blue Sea Visualization

Relax. You can relax your arms and legs by placing your hands on your stomach, heart chakra or knees. Be sure to wear comfortable clothes, but not too tight.

Allow yourself to be completely present. Do not allow your thoughts to enter your head. If you have any, just let them out and let them drift away like waves as they approach the lakeshore.

Waves slowly move in and out, one by one. Every thought should be in tune with the tides. Every emotion should go inwards and outwards.

Enjoy the moments of relaxation and take your time. You are free to be where you want to be.

At this moment, there is no one else to be. There is nothing that needs to be done at this time.

While your mind may drift to other thoughts, focus on the present experience.

Breathe deeply. Breathe positive energy. Breathe out love energy. Inhale negativity, then exhale anger energy. Do this three to 5 times per row.

It is a safe place where you can feel comfortable and at ease. Now, you're in a safe area where no one could ever hurt or harm you. This place is yours and only you can access it.

Do not hold onto any preconceived notions about what you should be doing. Accept yourself as you are. Allow the experience itself to flow naturally. Breathe at the pace that is most comfortable for you.

You can dive into the warm seawater. Feel the bubbles rise as you sink. Keep your gaze on the dolphins as you glide through the water.

As they sound off their language in the deep blue sea, you can hear the echoes. They communicate by diving deeper into the sea and back up again.

Feel the sunlight peeking through the liquid surface. Take a moment to enjoy the tranquility as you admire the pink coral. Other fish circle around you, passing by.

There is no better way of communicating than to feel your fingers touch their smooth skin. Unconditional love is the only thing that can be experienced.

Think about all the things in your head that you don't want to say. You are allowed to speak your mind and emotions. Let your voice be heard and remember that it's OK to speak out.

It doesn't matter if you keep your mouth shut. Dolphins are encouraging us to feel strong inside and to be bold enough for our opinions.

We've kept things inside too long. Others have made fun at us so we've been forced to keep our mouths shut. Because of the fear of being rejected, judged, ridiculed, or made fun of, we may believe that it isn't safe to speak our truths.

The deep blue sea will cleanse and wash away any fears that prevent you from speaking your truth. Be proud to be who you truly are.

Keep your convictions strong. Forgive anyone who does you harm through communication. Be kind to people who use hurtful language in communications.

Forgive yourself for being silent and for not setting boundaries. Relax and enjoy the tranquility of nature. Pay attention to what the dolphins have to say.

Let the sun shine on the water, and let it float you along. Once you reach the top of the mountain, take a deep breathe. As they wave goodbye, watch the dolphins leap in the air.

As long as you'd like, keep this feeling. When you're ready, you can stop this meditation at any time.

You can simply open your eyes. For a few seconds, relax, and then allow yourself to meditate.

Chapter 17: How To Find Your Creativity

Creativity has many interesting qualities. Momentous ideas can sometimes be referred to as 'increased mindfulness'. Sometimes, however, your creative flash may not be as successful as a Hanson profession. Creativity is vital, whether it is creating an ad campaign or coming up a new idea that could win the Loerie Award thought, Unfortunately, every once in a while the creative well goes dry. This is when we need to use methods to re-establish our creativity. Here are some ideas to help you tap into your creativity.

Exercise increases creativity

Exercise has more to do with well-being and health than it does for physical fitness. You are able to unleash your creative side. Researchers have found that exercise can enhance creativity. This is not difficult to believe, since exercise releases endorphins. Endorphins make us feel great. Feeling good makes it easier for you to think clever thoughts.

Keep Your Head Above the Water, But Don't Conform

You need to be able to understand your industry. It is important to understand your industry and not just follow others. It is important to get a basic understanding of the area's do's and don'ts. You can also understand patterns and guidelines, and then you can take them out when necessary. Your uniqueness will come from thinking in an unusual and practical way.

Travel

Travelling is like no other experience. You can expand your perspective, have fun and get out of your comfort zone. It's nothing like being introduced to new societies or people. This will assist you in restoring your innovative stream. It will give the mind a boost. Sometimes, travel can be expensive. Perhaps you could explore another part your city. It is a good idea to try and meet people from other walks of the life. You will find your inspiration.

Continue Writing Material

Creativity can be a bad habit. It tends to strike at the most inopportune times. Just when you need to have an in-house or shower epiphany. Keep some paper nearby to capture those musings. Always have at least one method to record a thought. There's nothing worse then coming up with something fantastic and then forgetting it.

Soft the Light

Many people love working in well-lit areas. However, researchers have found that it can increase creativity if there is less lighting. This is because dimming the light now and then gives you an unrestricted feeling. It can also be used to trigger an unconventional processing style.

There are many ways to inspire creativity

Inspiration can also be described as another way to solve an problem or answer an enquiry. It is easy to get bogged down by busyness and set examples in our lives. It is difficult to find creative answers to difficult questions. The following tips can help you to find inspiration and creativity whenever you feel the need. Depending on the situation, you can combine any or all of these ideas.

1. Change Your negative proclamation " I can't"

Sometimes our own personal settled examples can prove to be a major barrier to inspiration or creativity. Consider the issue: If you think too much about what you can or can't do, like "I don't know how..." or "I don't want to...", then you will likely make a negative selffulfilling prophecy and get stuck.

Instead, think instead of unfinished explanations or inquiries.

"I will find inspiration to understand it. "These open-ended explanations or inquiries will be your innovative mantras. Don't attempt to create answers by simply reciting them. Instead, allow your mind to wander.

2. Relax and enjoy Nature and the colors it offers

Nature and the colors of nature are well-known for their rejuvenating qualities. If you are feeling confused or need to gain clarity, try a space that has calming colors like green and blue. A bright environment like a garden or flower nursery can help you find new ideas. If you aren't ready to experience nature immediately, close the eyes and visualize it. You can see every season in your mind's eye; hear the sounds and smells of springs and winged animals; take in the outside environment. Let your body take in all the air you can while you rationally explore this beautiful environment. Visualize while listening to Mozart, or other enjoyable complex music. It's an enjoyable mental tour, and may be exactly what your mind needs to heal.

3. Check out Biographies Of Creative People Who Inspire You.

Can inspiration be transmitted? Completely! Watch or read the histories of creative people to help you find innovative arrangements.

4. Accept that your imagination is unlimited

Some people will exclaim that they are innovative, while others believe they were born with it. Others think you can't be creative and don't believe they have any. Everyone is capable of inventing, and experts have demonstrated that creativity can be developed through a variety of methods including diet, exercise, and practice. You can be imaginative, provided you have faith in yourself.

5. Find the wisdom in your deeper self

Releasing assumptions, habits, or examples. Don't think about what is possible or impossible. Meditating will allow you to connect to your deepest self. Accept the fact that you will need to hush for some time. Be open to new ideas and recognitions.

Expand your idea of who you really are. It is important that you acknowledge your true nature. You can also work with this. Inspire creativity from your true self.

Your more profound self will become wiser. You must let go of any notions that are limiting or impossible. Meditating will allow you to connect to your greater self. You can allow yourself normal times of quiet. Create space for new thoughts and recognitions.

6. Ask how to be of Service

Our higher self is unified in all of reality. Asking for advice on administration taps into this unity awareness, inviting it to view you through your eyes in service of all. This eliminates egotistical and narrow inspirations and addresses the force of infinity. Noiselessly ask yourself the following question: What would it take to help others? How can I help others?

7. Set your intentions

With full clarity and mindfulness, inspired creativity is easier to achieve. It is important to be clear about what you want. Be as specific as possible and confirm your intentions. Be clear about your intention and make sure you don't feel attached to the outcome.

8. Grasp your uniqueness

According to the spiritual Law of Dharma you are a unique focus of creative activity. This means that you have an original part to play and can be relied upon for inspiration. Recognize that there is a community of people who appreciate your inventive contributions.

9. Look at all obstacles as opportunities

Try to view all issues as opportunities. Every issue has win-win possibilities if you tap into your infinite creativity. These solutions ensure greater happiness, well-being and satisfaction for all. This is why you should search for all inclusive deals.

10. Achieve a level at which there are no problems

Problems are not present at the highest levels. Everything is perfect. You can create inspiring work at the highest possible levels by gaining this awareness in all situations.

Techniques for regaining your creativity

To gain creativity, your brain must learn how to address issues internally and not look for outside help. These are some powerful, yet simple ways to regain the creativity you have lost.

1. Be creative - Stop thinking about not being innovative and do.

What are your passions? What do your dreams look like? Start writing about these things, and you might be able to find another pursuit.

You have many options to unleash your innovative brain. Each route starts with self discovery

2. Move your body.

3. Recognize where you are at the moment - Do your skills allow you to cook? You can fix broken things. You can start a small garden. One of my most important lifelong interests is growing plants, writing, and cooking. In the past, however, I was a very active photographer. All are involved in creativity.

4. Add another skill to your repertoire - I have spent the last few years doing some home remodeling. This then led me into tile and mosaic making. It was mosaics where I found my love of color and glass.

5. Drawing or Diary: Writing sparks creativity. It ignites the right-brain area where your imagination is focused. Write and attract color. You'll be able to forget about the black pen and flawless handwriting, and discover hidden gifts.

Creative Thinking Skills Building Techniques

It's a talent that should be developed. People have the ability of being imaginative and able to create, outline, express, and communicate through many forms. It doesn't matter if you can quieten it or make use of that potential.

Children behave normally. They are generally able to accept rejection or judgement until their creative thoughts and expressions are hampered. They become aware of the fact that the world judges them and places needs on their creativity. The ability to think creatively is crucial for solving problems, organizing ideas, synthesizing or organizing information, as well as other tasks.

Two-fold task, once you've got it down.

1. Removing any obstructions to the procedure is possible

2. Begin to use methods that inspire creativity.

Easy.... right? However, what systems take expression into account and make ideas? Many of these "methods", in fact, may be best described as "methodologies" because they aren't very specialized. These are not a comprehensive list of enchantment methods. The truth is that the matter isn't as basic as it seems. It's impossible to program; it's hard to ensure; and it's not possible. It is essential to realize that these tools are meant to be used as a way to start the innovative stream. They are not mind pills.

They are innovative ways of approaching learning and teaching that promote innovation.

1. Perception

When we put our faculties into a center, and then rationally record what they find, we are processing information and also allowing ourselves the freedom to think about how that information fits in with what already exists and what it could be.

Perception can also be described as judgment and reason. A spot that can help us make arrangements is necessary when confronted with an issue. It is possible to create arrangements yourself by taking a step back and focusing.

Dan Meyer makes an astounding showing of explaining why giving an issue to understudies/youngsters, alongside the formula, hinders their ability to make solutions themselves. He also gives us a few examples of how he facilitates creative thinking in his classroom by using perception.

2. Analyse characteristic

This is a technique used to collect and explore substantial objects. You will take a camera or other item and list every property you can.

You can list parts, highlights and rewards as well. Ask addresses and you will be able to ask for suggestions on ways the item can be enhanced, combined with other things, simplified or phased out.

Imagine all the different ways the simple camera was modified over the years. Without innovative thinking, nobody would have put the camera in a cellphone, made it digital and made them waterproof or made them simple enough that even a child could use them.

3. Brainstorming

The purpose of brainstorming is to produce the most possible number of alternate ideas for future evaluation and advancement.

Judgment withheld until later

Create as many ideas and concepts as you can

Note the connections between ideas.

Combination of ideas and changes are encouraged

Quantity is the main theme here. While brainstorming can be a stressful process, it is important to have as many ideas as you can.

A mind map is an excellent way to encourage children to brainstorm ideas. There are many online tools available that can help both kids and grown-ups to create mind maps.

4. Imagination

We can process issues in our mind by using imaginative thought. Imagine possible results, situations and responses.

Then, they can become real. It is essential for cognitive enhancement and critical thinking.

Free-play is one way to get creative juices flowing. This is best taught in preschool classes that allow children to explore, play with and make their own ideas. Even adults and older children can use imagination to come up with new ideas.

By encouraging imagination during learning, you can create an opportunity for innovation by encouraging visualization and imagination.

5. Free Association

The concept of free association is similar in many ways to brainstorming. However, there is one significant difference. When you brainstorm, you're listing and compiling ideas. Free association allows you the freedom to concentrate on specific words or images.

What is the main word that you associate with the word "apple?" How about the word "apple" that you say? The idea behind free association is to inspire you to move beyond a topic and explore how things can be related.

You can also use this method for pictures. Draw a sketch or a basic picture. Take a look at your first picture and draw the photo you're most inspired by. Next, draw a photograph that can be identified as the one before it.

Chapter 18: Goals And Strategies For Success At Next Level

How to set and achieve personal goals

We practiced a mental exercise earlier. The mental exercise should have given us the best foundation for setting goals at different levels. It is the same procedure that we used to create smart goals. Let's examine a stepby-step guide to setting goals.

Step 1; To determine your professional and personal goals, first imagine the big picture. This is why you should call an internal meeting with your team and ask the following questions.

1. "What do you want out of your life?" Define clearly what you want from the time you have been given.

2. "What is it that you want me to achieve (large-scale targets) over the next five-10 years?

Step 2; Once you have a clear idea of the big picture', the long-term goals or large-scale, long-term goals, break them into smaller goals. This will allow you to work towards the larger goal. This will make it easier to achieve long-term, achievable goals in a shorter period of time. However, it's important to make sure the smaller goals you set are SMART (specific. measurable. achievable. realistic. and time bound). Importantly, for increased confidence and motivation, make it easy to accomplish the smaller goals.

Step 3 Step 3: Once your small smart goals are created (A smart goal is any goal that's "planned", i.e.

To achieve personal growth and goals, you must follow the three steps.

Tip. To be able to achieve the goals you have set for yourself and to make your life better, you need to practice positive affirmations. Positive affirmations are statements that will motivate you to take action towards the things you have in your life. These affirmations can be used to help you shift your mindset regarding different aspects of life.

Saying affirmations can help you accept challenges and motivate you to take action. You might say, for example, "I know what it takes to get the job done", "I have overcome any resistance to reaching my goals", "I will let pessimism fade away from my life", "My goals are in perfect harmony with my life", etc. Say it every day to your subconscious mind so it will believe it. You'll be able to transform your life if the subconscious believes that you can create what you feed it.

Summarizing success is to create, believe, and then get. Positive affirmations allow you to believe once you've conceived any ideas. Everything else will follow. Your goals must be POSITIVE STATEMENTS. Be sure to use present tense when writing affirmations. You should also make every affirmation positive and personal if your subconscious mind wants to believe it.

Note: It's possible to mix affirmations with things such as guided hypnosis, which can help you be more effective at what you do. Download MP3s, or look at YouTube videos for more information.

While this is a simplified version of setting goals, let's examine a few aspects of your personal success.

How to Set Lifetime Objectives

To grow yourself on any level, the first thing to do is think about your long-term objectives, i.e. determine your long-term achievements. This step is essential to setting achievable goals. It provides a wide-ranging perspective on your life. This long-term outlook can be used to influence your every-day decisions.

Your long term goals should be well-divided between all pillars in your life, and cover any area you deem to be important. The following categories should be included in your long-term goals: financial, career, family, and spiritual.

Your life can be greatly affected by long-term goals. Therefore, it is important to brainstorm goals in every category and pick the best goal that covers what you desire with a specific pillar in your life.

Be sure to set your own goals for each pillar. This will ensure you are not being forced to follow the example of your spouse, parent, or other family members.

Tips: Our tips have shown you that smart goals are the best goals. Setting smart goals is difficult. These guidelines should make it easier.

1. Goals should be expressed as positive affirmations. You must remember that motivation and personal growth come with positive charge. Your goals should be positive charged.

2. List your goals. If you write your goals down on a piece if paper, it gives them the

emotional power and power to be realized in your life.

3. Smaller goals should always be manageable and simple. The achievement of an operational goal (goals you're currently working at) becomes much easier when it is easier. But, if you have a large operational goal, it can discourage you and cause you to believe you aren't getting anywhere.

4. Smaller goals can be more distinctive. You can achieve distinction by setting time limitations and achievement criteria for your goals. This will increase the urgency of the goal (personal success or excellence should be urgent). This will drive you towards specific goals, and reward you by giving you confidence and motivation to pursue other goals.

5. Prioritize: After setting your long term goals, prioritise each goal. You should complete the most important goal first. This will prevent you from feeling overworked.

6. OUTCOME GAMES ARE NOT TO BE SET. They are goals that are dependent upon something or someone else. Your goal list should contain only goals that you have some control over. Your goals should not be based on outcome goals. Instead, consider using your personal performance to guide you. This allows you to have total control over the accomplishment of your goals.

If you've set goals for your entire life in each pillar of the world, then it's time to break those goals down into smaller ones. Let's begin.

How to Set Smaller Objectives

After brainstorming goals that span different pillars of life, and then selecting one goal that represents what you want to accomplish in that area, the next thing is to trim that goal down to create smaller goals that are easier for you to understand and reach.

It is crucial to take into consideration the length of your long-term goal when breaking them down. To illustrate, once you've identified long-term goals create a plan detailing their duration. Consider, for example, what you would like to achieve in the next five decades. You can then break down your five-year plan into six-month plans. Three-month plans. A 6-month plan. One month plans. One week plans. Daily plans.

To help you achieve your lifetime goals, make a To-Do List of daily actions plans. This will give you a lot of insight into what your first set if goals should be. It is important to review and keep this To-Do List updated every day.

What to do once you have achieved smaller goals

You can take a few moments to reflect on how you feel about reaching your goals after you accomplish them.

Note: If you accomplish a goal, or reach an achievement, you feel euphoric. This has a huge positive effect on your motivation and ability to achieve other goals. The euphoric feeling gives you confidence that you can achieve anything you want.

If you achieve a set of goals that have a lot of meaning to the end goal of the goal, reward yourself with the best way you can. Take some time to reflect on the goal, even though you are rejoicing yourself. Take for example the achievement of the goal. Was the task easy? If it was, you can make the next goal harder. Did it take longer to achieve the goal? If so make the next one shorter and simpler. Did you learn something that could have an impact on other goals or was it beneficial? If so, you can change your other goals to reflect your insights.

What to do when you fail to achieve your goals

It's not acceptable to let failure to reach goals or meet deadlines be something that you resentfully ignore. There has never been a better saying: determination is having the faith and motivation that you will persevere, even when it seems hopeless.

There are many choices you have when it comes to what you do, if and how you fail to accomplish your goals. You can choose to accept the negative consequences of failure in your life or procrastinate through your goals. This will make them seem impossible. However, this could also be used as a reference point to guide your determination to achieve the next or more important goal.

It is impossible to give you a plan or tell you what to do when you fail at your goals. But here are some things that you shouldn't do.

Never give up. Remember that personal development requires courage and determination to be your best (personal excellence).

The foundation of personal development is the setting of goals. It is also important to mention that, although setting goals and achieving them is key to eliminating procrastination is not the only thing that matters.

Tip 2: Get rid of negative self-talk. It is impossible to succeed if your mind keeps telling you how difficult it is or how incompetent you are at getting things done. Don't forget to be your own cheerleader. You're the only one who can help you succeed. If your inner critic constantly tells you that your goals are impossible, you will likely settle in your current status quo. If you continue to follow the same path as your previous one, you will not be able to achieve anything. Make a list that is positive about you and state positive affirmations regarding your life and the tasks ahead. By doing this, you can feel better about your life overall and the tasks that are at hand. In fact, for every negative thing you say about yourself, think of five positive affirmations that will help to neutralize those negative thoughts. You might also want to challenge any negative thoughts your inner critic may bring up. It is possible to ask for evidence that your inner critic has brought up about the goal. For example, if your inner critic is saying that "I don't know what it takes" then tell it to list 10 reasons why.

It is important to stop having negative thoughts even if you don't achieve the goals that you set. If you do, you will not be able or willing to move forward. Such negative thoughts include:

Catastrophizing

Negative psychic patterns, i.e. Mind Reading

Generalizing

This is the worst kind of thinking: You think everything is terrible.

Unsubstantiated   conclusive   thought patterns

All your mistakes are your own.

Your emotions should take control of your thinking

An all-or nothing mentality

Can, should, will, must mentality

The only way to see things is in black and/or white. You can't have success or failure if you don't look at the average.

Finding problems even in situations without them

Accepting credit only when things go well and not taking responsibility for any negatives

Believe you can control anything

Starter optimism: This is underestimating how long it would take for an unfamiliar task to be completed.

Insisting on a poor performance to transform everything

Your thinking can be poisoned by envy

In the next chapter we will talk about spiritual growth. This chapter will help you to reach your goals and give you tips on spiritual growth.

Chapter 19: Imagination Or Willpower

Willpower is designed to fail.

Ever tried to relax in a nervous setting? The more you try, you will fail. Some lucky people have learned how to take deep breathes and imagine something relaxing and humorous as though they were naked. Many people cannot relax, and will continue to live their whole lives.

Willpower is an ability that your brain was designed to provide you with an easy way for your brain to disregard your orders. Most of the times, it is doing so for your own benefit, or the betterment of the human race. For example, a man who tells his partner not have an orgasm will most likely make it happen twice faster. It is common to consider baseball or any other non-sexual subject as a way to delay orgasm.

The mind reacts to what the believe, and not what the will. If you believe something your mind will go to every extent to make it true. That could include changing your perceptions and changing the world around yourself.

As I mentioned at beginning of the book, I have read numerous self-help and motivational books during my research for this novel. One thing unites them all is to be conscious of your thoughts and focus on positive thoughts. I've tried this but with little success. To change my thinking, I have had some success with noticing what I was doing and then saying "cancel" "cancel".

It was then that I realized our beliefs play a significant role in what we believe and how we feel about the things happening in our lives. My beliefs were always in harmony with the thoughts that just came my way. If I was given new information, either my self-talk (or my logical head) would interpret it according to the beliefs of my belief system. It became more difficult when it became apparent that many of the beliefs I hold are a result my "imprint", years, and were not conscious.

Even if a belief doesn't seem resourceful, I wouldn't know it.

All I would notice is the results. It took me a while to realize that I "acted in a particular way" to have a home where guests were invited but not for my enjoyment. While I enjoy being with friends and feeling at home in my home, it was clear to me that I would need to change myself to get the results I desire in other areas. I then began to research belief and imagination. When I changed my beliefs, my thoughts immediately changed.

"If your keep doing the same thing as you have always done, it's a good idea."

You will always have what you had always been"

Belief or Imagination? "I"ll Believe It When I See It!" Or I'll only see it if I believe it.

Please Pay Attention to This Part of the Book! !

The subconscious mind, also known as our habitual subconscious computer, directs our every day actions and reactions.

We must make some changes in our unconscious beliefs about ourselves if we want to see positive results in our lives. We can use this scramble pattern to resolve any negative emotions that may be arising from a situation now or in the past.

How do we change these subconscious beliefs? Let's go over how the mind works. When we ask a question or need to know the solution to a problem, our conscious minds check the memory banks of the unconscious and return an answer in nanoseconds. This could be a thought, or just a feeling. Many of our responses are automatic. It is possible to drive a car if you are used to it. Your unconscious mind can then do it for you. This is because our reactions are automatic, and we don't need to think. (Most of the time, our unconscious minds record images, feelings, and sounds and operate about 95% or more of our actions.

Up until now, it was difficult to get an update in the answers we received from our unconscious databases. Additionally, since we kept getting similar responses from our databanks, we would "act in this way" or react in predictable ways when faced with a given situation.

You do not have to recognize and change all of your imprinted emotions, thoughts, and memories if you are looking for different results. You don't need to lie down and find all your limiting beliefs. Researchers have found that only new information is required to be added to your unconscious data bank. If there were fresh new experiences to build on top, the answer to the situation questions would be different. It would lead to different actions.

For example, if you believe that you cannot run a 4-minute mile, then your data bank (unconscious mind), will tell you so. Your data banks can record a 4-minute mile as a belief. If you actually do run it, you'll believe it can be done again. If you see someone running a four-minute marathon, your rational consciousness will believe that you can do it too. However, your beliefs may prevent you from trying.

It was believed that we must have the new experience in order to alter our unconscious data bank. You could also submit the idea directly to your conscious reasoning mind. If it proved true, then you would record it as true. Your reasoning brain may conclude that your ideas are false, and it will be recorded accordingly. (The four minute mile is not in question.

Your reasoning mind was unable to believe that you were okay, as your imprinted data bank had other information.

Everything changed after we learned how to get the desired information into our unconscious minds. The first person to run four-minute miles was the one who "saw" himself doing so. Brainwaves couldn't be scientifically measured until the importance and significance of picturing was discovered. He saw himself running a marathon in a time everyone thought impossible. It was because it had never been done previously. Keep reading to find out how difficult it is to change a belief with only conscious reasoning.

This is the way that the reasoning or conscious head works.

It has been shown that the conscious mind will return a negative response the first time we present an idea to it. This is because the subconscious data banks do not contain any information, so the answer to our question is either no or I don't believe so.

The second time, though, the answer is still "no", but not as emphatically.

Third time around, it might be: I have heard it before, but not yet.

Fourth time, the answer to that question is "I know a lot" (The idea appears to be showing up in recordings searches.

Fifth time, I replied that I always knew this

The person will listen six times to the idea and then tell his friends.

Advertisers know this process well and that is why we see similar commercials over-and-over.

Over the years, most people have found it difficult to maintain their willpower and change their imprinted beliefs. Although the repetition technique to learn was used to make us purchase things, it was not obvious that it was happening. It was more like boiling water for a frog. Have you ever considered boiling a frog. Learn by listening. He will run away if you boil water the frog. You can put the frog in cold water with the burner turned on and he will stay there until the water boils. It is so easy to boil the frog. Listening to repetitive ads can lead us to be like the frog.

How does subconscious learning convert to conscious learning?

Let me first say that some of our unconscious beliefs refer to tribal beliefs or beliefs that are held within the family, community, extended family and close friends. It is a common belief that one must work hard in order to succeed in this society. We are taught from a young age to never dream of becoming a millionaire. Many of the things we learn in school are roted or repeated.

We are expected to do the same as our bosses, which is to work hard and conform. Ninety percent of us will find work and are satisfied with our "job". We settle for "good enough" and take care of the families.

On the one hand, we go and pray and the Holy Scriptures says that "whenever ye believe, ye may have it and we'll sell it to ye." It just says you shall have it... or, as Saint Augustine (345-430), Theologian/Bishop said, "faith refers to the ability to believe something that you do not see. And to "see" yourself well even when you are not. "Seeing yourself happy" when you aren't, "seeing the best in yourself, no matter your present circumstances, and "seeing it with the love" of your life. You were born with imagination. However, your childhood was also shaped to believe imagination was impossible. The visible truth that hard work pays off in your life was something your parents, grandparents and aunts, uncles rely on (money doesn't grow from trees you know). It was called daydreaming, because imagination did not have any direct benefits that could easily be seen.

Abraham Lincoln (1809-1865).

Wisdom is timeless. It says your imagination, or the ability to believe in things you can't, is more powerful then muscle.

You may be surprised to see that belief quotes do not speak of the afterlife. These quotes are about the now. After reading this book, you will have a better understanding of how to let your imagination run wild. It worked miracles for Saint Augustine and Jesus.

The brains of both our sides. Modern psychology recognizes the fact that both parts of our consciousness make up our personality. However, we typically only have access one of these sides. During the day our conscious mind governs, and when we sleep, our unconscious minds take control. Dreams create new worlds in our minds and transform ordinary objects into the extraordinary, the fantastic and sometimes the terrifying. We see reality differently. There are numerous examples from history that show individuals who can retain some conscious activity during nightly dreams. This activity has been extensively explored over the past 40-50 years. To describe it, the term "Lucid Dreaming" is used.

What is Lucid Dreaming, exactly?

Frederik Van Eeden, a Dutch psychiatrist originally coined the term. The Dutch psychiatrist defined it as "mental clearness".

Lucid Dreams refer to a dream in that the dreamer becomes aware of the fact that he/she is dreaming. This allows the dreamer to manipulate the dream's events. Lucid Dreams trigger a brain part responsible for self awareness - the Dorsolateral Prefrontal Cortex, if I'm not mistaken! Not only does it give you control over the dream, but it also allows access to a hidden part of your consciousness that is usually not possible. Lucid Dreaming simply means that both sides of our brains can be active at the same moment.

Most people will experience a Lucid Dream some day in their lives. Some experience them every day, others only occasionally. While many people recall their dreams vividly, others aren't able to remember what happened during the dream. Some people forget about their dreams completely. It is possible to have lucid dreams. This book will explain the steps and techniques you can use to get into your dreams. Lucid Dreaming also has some practical benefits.

Lucid Dreaming Basics

Lucid Dream can be confusing. Before we discuss the benefits and techniques it is important to know what Lucid Dream is.

Lucid Dreaming can be described as being awake but not fully awake. Lucid Dreaming occurs when you are in the REM phase of sleep.

Lucid Dreaming can also be confused sometimes with what is called an "outof body experience" (or Astral Projection). These experiences usually refer to events happening outside of the mind. They are the ability to be present with the real world using what is called our Astral Body. Lucid Dreaming can be experienced in one's own head.

Lucid dream can be extremely vivid, but not in the same way as vivid dreams. Lucid Dreams can be very vivid and you will not be aware of it. A vivid dream may seem real, but your conscious mind will wake up and realize that it is all a dream.

Lucid Dreaming can help you access both sides of your consciousness. This state allows you the opportunity to "meet" aspects of yourself and your psychology that aren't normally available. These parts often show up as people. This allows you to have deep and extremely valuable conversations, which can help you learn about yourself.

CPSIA information can be obtained
at www.ICGtesting.com
Printed in the USA
BVHW052247090223
658263BV00007B/249

9 781774 856291